Better Homes and Gardens®

COUNTRY CHRISTMAS CRAFTS

BETTER HOMES AND GARDENS® BOOKS

Editor: Gerald M. Knox
Art Director: Ernest Shelton
Managing Editor: David A. Kirchner
Project Editors: James D. Blume, Marsha Jahns
Project Managers: Liz Anderson,
    Jennifer Speer Ramundt, Angela K. Renkoski

Crafts Editor: Sara Jane Treinen
Senior Crafts Editors: Beverly Rivers,
    Patricia M. Wilens
Associate Crafts Editor: Nancy Reames

Associate Art Directors: Neoma Thomas,
    Linda Ford Vermie, Randall Yontz
Assistant Art Directors: Lynda Haupert,
    Harijs Priekulis, Tom Wegner
Graphic Designers: Mary Schlueter Bendgen,
    Michael Burns, Brenda Lesch
Art Production: Director, John Berg;
    Associate, Joe Heuer;
    Office Manager, Michaela Lester

President, Book Group: Jeramy Lanigan
Vice President, Retail Marketing: Jamie L. Martin
Vice President, Administrative Services: Rick Rundall

BETTER HOMES AND GARDENS® MAGAZINE
President, Magazine Group: James A. Autry
Editorial Director: Doris Eby

MEREDITH CORPORATION OFFICERS
Chairman of the Executive Committee: E. T. Meredith III
Chairman of the Board: Robert A. Burnett
President: Jack D. Rehm

COUNTRY CHRISTMAS CRAFTS
Editor: Beverly Rivers
Editorial Project Manager: Jennifer Speer Ramundt
Graphic Designer: Mary Schlueter Bendgen
Electronic Text Processor: Paula Forest

Cover projects: See pages 50–51 and 158.

From a rustic log cabin to a slick city condominium, the wonderful handmade decorations in **Country Christmas Crafts** will help you get ready for a good old-fashioned holiday, country-style.

Nothing compares to the excitement and traditions of a family Christmas. The hustle and bustle surrounding the tree decorating and the making of personal gifts seems to spark everyone's spirits early in the season.

Country Christmas Crafts will provide you with fresh ideas for dolls, samplers, afghans, quilts, and other country trimmings that will delight friends and family.

CONTENTS

A Taste of Country Christmas

No matter where you live, you can celebrate a country Christmas by turning simple materials into holiday treasures. Here, and on the next four pages, is a peek at the kinds of festive ideas you'll find throughout this book.

Traditional quilt patterns add color and pastoral charm to the Christmas gifts and decorations found here.

Festive red and green fabrics and basic quilting techniques are used to create the poinsettia table runner, *right*. The floral motifs are appliquéd to a muslin background and centered between two pieced star panels.

Use the leftover fabric scraps to machine- or hand-stitch the child's pine tree collar. Worn over a dress sewn from a commercial pattern, the collar slips over the head and measures 11 inches from the shoulder to the Empire waistline.

Instructions and patterns for the projects in this chapter begin on page 12.

Spruce up your kitchen with a tree trimmed in a generous helping of cooking utensils and tart pan ornaments, *right*. Mix up a batch of these goodies using felt fabric and purchased appliqués, and glue them to the insides of tart pans. Embellish the hearts and wreaths with beads and ribbon bows.

Use red or green ribbons to tie small kitchen scoops, cookie cutters, whisks, and graters to the pine branches. (Best to choose utensils that are lightweight.)

A pine cupboard may be the perfect place to display a pair of painted wooden Santas like those, *opposite*. Make these rustic Santas and their sacks of goodies with scraps of wood, muslin, and twine. Use acrylic paints and antiquing glaze to give the figures their old-fashioned appeal. Fill the bags with cinnamon sticks and spices to create a fragrance reminiscent of Grandma's holiday desserts.

The woolly trio of hand-knitted stockings, *right,* is bursting with surprises from Mr. and Mrs. Claus. Measuring from top to tippy-toe, each stocking is about 24 inches long.

Although both are quick and easy to make, the cross-stitched gifts, *opposite,* will surely be cherished by friends and family for years to come.

The photo mat is worked with red and green floss on perforated paper. The simple repetition of hearts is a snap to stitch.

And, the mini-sampler, stitched on 14-count Aida cloth, definitely relays a message that we all endorse, that friendship is truly the best gift of all.

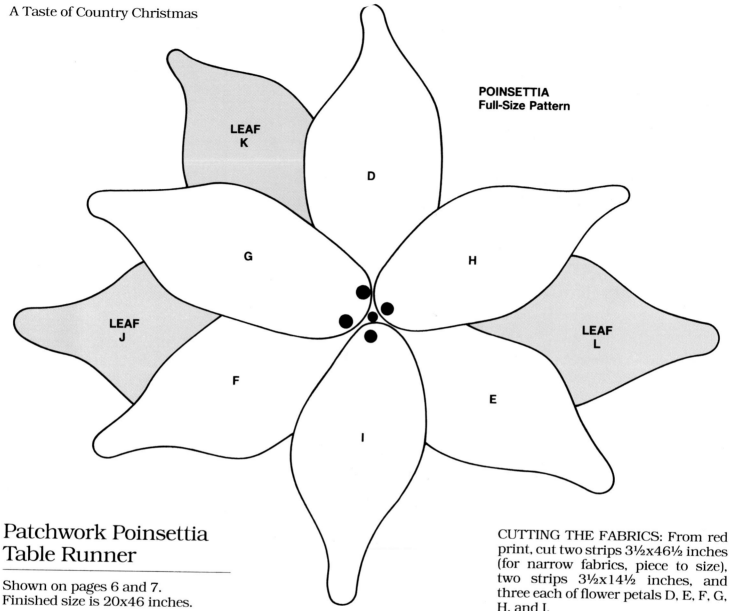

**POINSETTIA
Full-Size Pattern**

LEAF
K

D

G

H

LEAF
J

LEAF
L

F

E

I

Patchwork Poinsettia Table Runner

Shown on pages 6 and 7.
Finished size is 20x46 inches.

MATERIALS
¾ yard of red print fabric
¼ yard of green dot or print fabric
1½ yards of muslin fabric
¼ yard of red solid fabric
1 skein gold embroidery floss
24x50 inches of batting

INSTRUCTIONS
The pattern, *above,* is full size. Diagrams, *opposite,* will help you determine layout of pieces. Add ⅛-inch seam allowance before cutting out.

MAKING STAR TEMPLATES: Cut templates from cardboard or plastic. To make Template B, cut a 3-inch square. The triangle for Template A is one-half of the 3-inch square, cut on the diagonal. (See Diagram B, *opposite.*) Cut a 4¼-inch square for Template C.

Trace around templates on wrong side of fabric to mark pieces. Add ¼-inch seam allowances when cutting out the shapes.

CUTTING THE FABRICS: From red print, cut two strips 3½x46½ inches (for narrow fabrics, piece to size), two strips 3½x14½ inches, and three each of flower petals D, E, F, G, H, and I.

From green dot or print, cut four strips 1½x12½ inches, two strips 1½x40½ inches, one J leaf, three K leaves, and three L leaves.

From muslin, cut a backing rectangle 20½x46½ inches (cut fabric lengthwise), one 12½-inch square for the poinsettia block, 24 A pieces, and eight B pieces.

From the red solid fabric, cut 16 A and two C pieces.

PIECING THE DESIGN: Diagrams A and B, *opposite,* will help you deter-

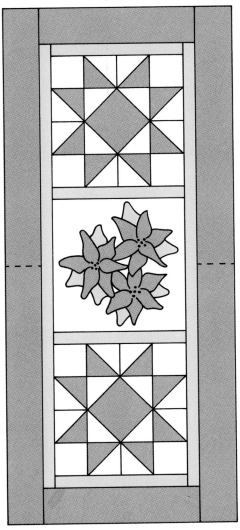

DIAGRAM A

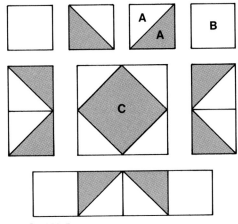

DIAGRAM B

FINISHING THE RUNNER: Use ¼-inch seams for all sewing.

Referring to Diagram A, join the blocks with green latticework adding four horizontal strips, followed by two long vertical strips.

To make the outer border, stitch the 3½x14½-inch red strips to short ends of table runner. Add 3½x46½-inch borders to long sides of runner.

Press runner on back side. Center on top of batting and backing. Baste together. Quilt as desired.

Finish table runner with self-made or commercial binding. (Yardage for red print allows adequate fabric for self-made binding.)

Christmas Collar

Shown on pages 6 and 7. Finished size of collar shown is 11 inches wide with 11-inch drop from shoulder to Empire waistline.

MATERIALS
½ yard of red print fabric
½ yard of green print fabric
¼ yard of muslin
Scrap of black fabric for tree trunks
½ yard of backing fabric

mine layout of pieces. Piece two star blocks following Diagram B.

Machine- or hand-appliqué the poinsettia block referring to Diagram A, *above*, and the photograph on pages 6 and 7 for leaf and petal placement. Complete flower centers by making five French knots for each flower using three strands of gold embroidery floss.

3 yards of 1-inch-wide green ribbon for sides
2 yards of ⅝-inch green ribbon for back
12x24-inch batting

INSTRUCTIONS
The patterns, *below*, are full size. Diagram A on page 14 will help you determine layout of pieces.

CUTTING THE PIECES: Trace the full-size patterns on cardboard or plastic to make templates. Trace around the template on the wrong side of the fabric to mark pieces. Add ¼-inch seam allowances when cutting out the shapes.

continued

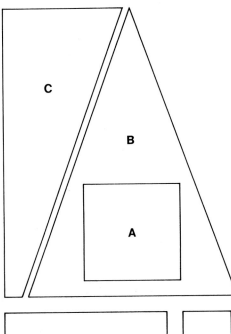

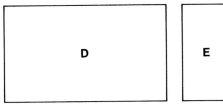

CHRISTMAS COLLAR
Full-Size Patterns

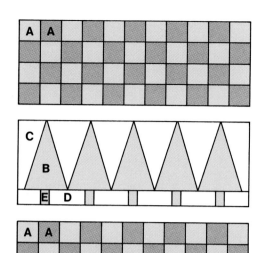

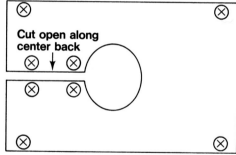

DIAGRAM A

DIAGRAM B

Repeat for collar back. Join pieced halves to form one long rectangle. (The collar opening will be cut later.)

FINISHING THE COLLAR: Layer the pieced collar, batting, and backing; baste layers together. Cut neck opening as shown in Diagram B, *left*, making the opening 1 inch larger all the way around than the neck opening of the dress or blouse. Quilt collar by hand or machine "in the ditch" around trees, trunks, and squares.

Baste wide ribbon ties in place at collar sides and narrow ribbon ties at collar back. Ribbon location is designated by the X markings on Diagram B. Bind the collar with commercial bias.

Wooden Santas

Shown on page 9.
Finished sizes are 10½ inches tall (small) and 14 inches tall (large).

MATERIALS
4x6-inch fir (28-inch length makes both sizes)
¼-yard muslin scraps (for sack)
Graphite paper
⅛-inch dowel and drill bit
Sphagnum moss
Twine
Black, white, and flesh paints
Fiberfill
Gesso
Small and large artist's brushes
Matte-finish varnish

For Santa's toys and trees
Scraps of ⅜-inch birch plywood
Green, tan, brown, and blue acrylic paint

INSTRUCTIONS
For the Santas
The pattern, *above right* and *opposite*, is full size for the small Santa.

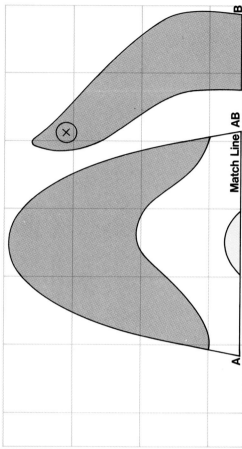

WOODEN SANTAS

Collar, as shown, will fit child from Size 5 or 6 to Size 8. For the smaller collar, subtract one tree and two vertical rows of checkerboard squares. For longer collar, increase the rows of horizontal squares.

Cut fabrics as follows: From red print, cut 76 A pieces. Use remainder of red for binding.

From green print, cut 76 A and 10 B pieces. From muslin, cut eight B, four C, and 12 D pieces.

From black fabric, cut 10 E pieces. From the backing fabric, cut a 13x24-inch rectangle.

PIECING THE COLLAR: Piece collar front as shown in Diagram A, *above*.

To make the larger Santa, enlarge the pattern to the scale given. (Match pattern lines A and B to join the pattern sections together.)

Cut body shape from 4x6-inch fir. Cut arms and tree from plywood.

Drill ⅛-inch holes on the body and each arm and on the trees as marked by the circled X on the pattern.

Sand all pieces smooth.

Using graphite paper, transfer the body and arm markings to the appropriate pieces. Paint all areas with acrylic paint, allowing ample drying time between colors. Use gesso to texture Santa's beard. Dab a light touch of red to the cheek area.

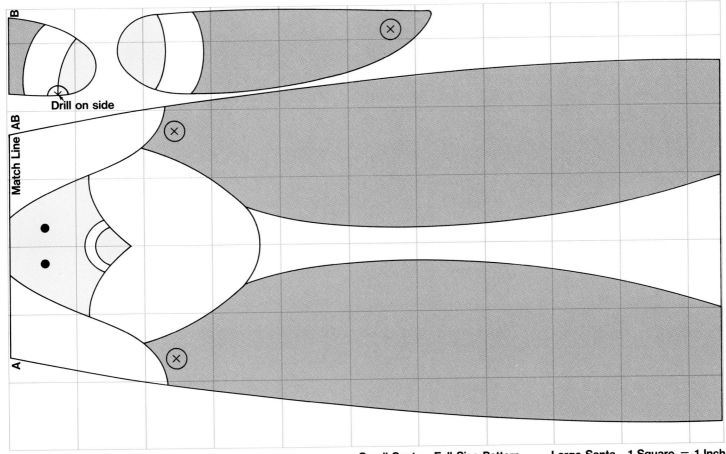

B

Drill on side

Match Line AB

A

Small Santa - Full-Size Pattern Large Santa - 1 Square = 1 Inch

Paint the Christmas tree green.

Sand the painted Santa and tree. Coat with antiquing glaze. Let glaze set a few minutes; wipe excess glaze from Santa using a soft cloth.

Using the end of small artist's brush and black paint, make two dots for Santa's eyes.

Spray entire Santa and tree with matte-finish varnish.

Cut the dowel into three ½-inch pieces. Join tree to Santa's hand using a piece of dowel. Join arms to body using remaining two pieces of dowel. Glue moss onto white area of Santa's hood.

Cut muslin into a 6x12-inch rectangle. Fold in half to make a piece that measures 6x6 inches and sew raw edges together, leaving one short end open. Turn right side out. Hem open end inward to form a ½-inch casing, leaving an opening to insert twine. Thread twine through casing. Knot ends together and tie around Santa's arm. (Refer to the photograph on page 9 for guidance.) Fill the bottom of the bag with cinnamon and spices, potpourri, or fiberfill. Add painted plywood toys. Pull twine to gather top of sack.

For the toys

Cut doll and horse shapes from plywood. Paint with acrylic paints. Finish with matte-finish varnish.

Glue twine to the horse for a tail. Glue yarn to the doll's head for hair.

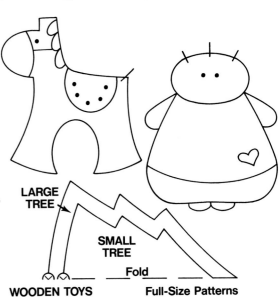

LARGE TREE

SMALL TREE

Fold

WOODEN TOYS Full-Size Patterns

15

Tart Pan Ornaments

Shown on pages 6–8.

MATERIALS

Tart pans in round and heart
shapes (available at cooking
supply shops)
Red and white scraps of felt
Green print fabric
Purchased heart and flower
appliqués
3 mm silver-plated beads
Red seed beads
Red embroidery floss
Crewel wool yarns in dark and
light greens
Red and green grosgrain ribbons

INSTRUCTIONS

Enlarge the patterns, *right,* onto paper. Cut out the pattern pieces. Cut
shapes from felt, referring to the
photograph on page 8 for colors.

For the heart ornament, cut two
large hearts and one small heart. For
the round ornament, cut two round
shapes and one wreath shape.

Appliqué the smaller heart or the
wreath to the appropriate background. Referring to page 186, stitch
the two large round shapes or the
two larger heart shapes together using the blanket stitch, leaving an
opening for stuffing. Stuff shapes
firmly; stitch opening closed.

Hand-sew the purchased heart appliqué to the heart ornament.

Embroider evergreen branches on
the heart ornament using the featherstitch and two strands of green
yarn. (Stitch diagram appears on
page 186.) Sew the 3-mm silver
beads onto the branches. Add a
small green bow.

Sew three red seed beads onto
wreath. Attach bow. (Refer to photograph on page 8 for placement.)

Use a hammer and nail to make
two holes, side-by-side, in the top of
the tart pan. Thread ribbon through

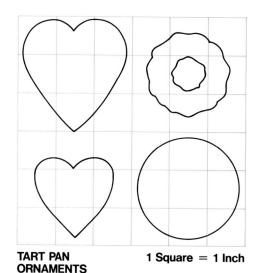

TART PAN ORNAMENTS   **1 Square = 1 Inch**

the holes for hanging. Put several
heavy dots of crafts glue in the bottom of the tart pan. Glue the ornament in place inside of the tart pan.
Allow the glue to dry.

Red-and-White Striped Stocking

Shown on page 10.
Finished size is 24½ inches long.

MATERIALS

Brown Sheep Top-of-the-Lamb
worsted weight (4-ounce skein):
one skein *each* of No. 420 red
and No. 100 white
One set of Size 8 double-pointed
knitting needles or size to reach
gauge given below

Gauge: 17 sts = 4 inches.

INSTRUCTIONS

With red, cast on 48 sts; join, taking
care not to twist work. Work 14 rnds
k 1, p 1 ribbing.

EYELET RND: * K 2 tog, yo; rep from
* around. Work 7 rnds more. Work
from Chart 1, *above,* for 70 rnds.

Chart 1   **Chart 2**

☒ Red   ◯ White

1 Square = 1 Stitch

HEEL OPENING: *Rnd 1:* With fourth
needle in pat, k across 12 sts of first
needle. Sl last 12 sts from third needle onto other end of fourth needle.
(Note: Fourth needle becomes first
needle (24 sts). Divide between second and third needle rem 24 sts.
Complete round.

Next rnd: Drop main colors of
yarn. With contrasting color of yarn,
k across first 24 sts of rnd. Drop contrasting yarn. Pick up main colors of
yarn and k in pat across first 24 sts
again. Complete rnd.

FOOT: Continue with chart pat as
established for 25 rnds. Drop white
and work toe with red.

TOE: Dec for toe as follows:
Rnd 1: K 1, sl 1, k 1, psso, k to
within 3 sts of end of first needle, k 2
tog, k 1; second needle: k 1, sl 1, k 1,
psso, k to end of second needle; third
needle: K to within 3 sts of end of
third needle. K 2 tog, k 1.

Next rnd: Work even. Rep these
two rounds until 16 sts rem.k 1, sl 1,
k 1, psso, k to end of rnd.

NEXT ROUND: Work even. Rep 2
rnds until 16 sts rem. Slip 4 rem sts
from third to second needle. Join
rem 16 sts using kitchener stitch.

HEEL: Remove contrast yarn at heel
opening; sl 24 lps below opening to
needle, divide 23 lps above opening
on 2 needles, picking up 1 st at corner of opening—48 sts. Shape as for
toe. Block stocking. Sew side seam.

Turn hem facing to inside along
eyelet row. Sew in place with matching yarn. Make yarn loop hanger on
inside of hem. Trim as desired.

Red-and-White Patterned Stocking

Shown on page 10.
Finished size is 22½ inches long.

MATERIALS

Nature Spun Yarns 3-ply worsted
(4-ounce skein): one skein *each*
of No. 740 white and No. 210 red
Size 8 double-pointed knitting
needles

Gauge: Over pattern st, 5 sts = 1
inch.

INSTRUCTIONS

With white, cast on 48 sts; join.
Work 10 rnds, eyelet rnd, then work
2 rnds; beg Chart 2, *opposite right,*
and work 74 rnds. Work heel opening as for Red-and-White Striped
Stocking. Continue Chart 2 for foot
until 26 rnds are completed. Break
off red. Work white toe as for Red-
and-White Striped Stocking toe.
Complete as for Red-and-White
Striped Stocking, with white heel.

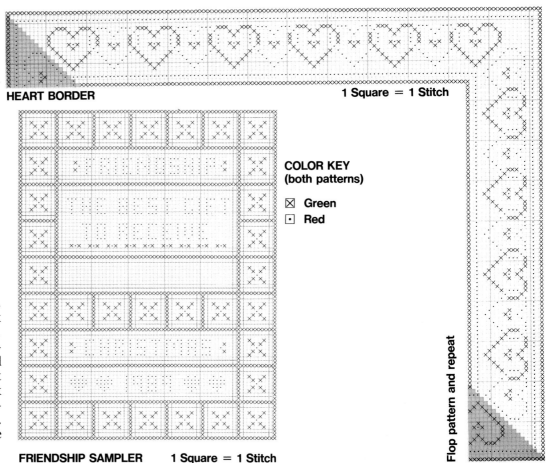

HEART BORDER

1 Square = 1 Stitch

**COLOR KEY
(both patterns)**

⊠ **Green**

⊡ **Red**

Flop pattern and repeat

FRIENDSHIP SAMPLER   **1 Square = 1 Stitch**

Green-and-Red Striped Stocking

Shown on page 10.
Finished size is 22½ inches long.

MATERIALS

Nature Spun Yarns 3-ply worsted
(4-ounce skein): one skein *each*
of No. 210 red and No. 501 green
Size 8 double-pointed knitting
needles

Gauge: Over pat st, 9 sts = 2
inches.

INSTRUCTIONS

With green, cast on 48 sts; join.
Work 14 rnds, then work eyelet rnd;
work 12 rnds green, then work (8
rnds red, 8 rnds green) four times.
Work heel opening as for Red-and-
White Striped Stocking.

FOOT: Work 8 rnds green, 8 rnds
red, then 8 rnds green. Break off
green. Complete toe as for Red-and-
White Striped Stocking using red.
Work heel with red; complete as for
Red-and-White Striped Stocking.

Friendship Sampler And Picture Mat

Shown on page 11.
Finished size of design on Friendship sampler is 5x6½ inches. Heart
mat design measures 7x8½ inches.

MATERIALS

8x9½-inch piece of 14-count Aida
cloth for sampler; 10x11½-inch
piece of perforated paper for mat
Embroidery floss in green and red
Embroidery needle
Sewing scissors

INSTRUCTIONS

Transfer the pattern(s), *above,* onto
graph paper. Or, work directly from
our pattern(s).

   For both stitcheries, use three
plies of floss and stitch over one
square of fabric or paper.

   Frame as desired. (For the mat-
ting, use sharp scissors to cut the
center to fit your photograph.)

A Friendly Welcome

Trim the tree, deck the halls, and get ready for a joyous country Christmas celebration. Handmade ornaments, wreaths, and wall hangings in this chapter will put you in the mood.

S pring and summer flowers, dried and saved from the season past, create a beautiful counterpoint to winter's snowdrifts and icicles.

Tucked into clear glass Christmas balls, the potpourri shines through in pinks, lavenders, and other wonderful pastels.

Press flowers behind the glass of miniature picture frames and add a satin ribbon for hanging.

Embellish tiny straw hats purchased from a crafts store with small dried flowers or strawflowers and moss.

Instructions for all projects in this section begin on page 24.

For many families, Christmas is a sentimental reminder of past celebrations. Newly crafted treasures take their places among old favorites.

The mantel, *opposite,* is decorated with trims torn from fabric scraps: a rag garland, the word "joy," and a rag heart. The stocking on the mantel and the whimsical angel guarding the hearth are machine-stitched in reverse appliqué.

The 15¾x20¾-inch framed sampler features a handsome border of 14 different quilt motifs translated into cross-stitch.

A FRIENDLY WELCOME

If you love country-style decorating, you're probably the kind of family that has a cherished collection of one kind or another. The elements within the collection do not have to be old or valuable to be desirable. They are simply things that make you feel good, and provide a common point of interest for the family during vacations, antique hunts, or shopping sprees.

Here, and on the opposite page, are some ideas for sharing your favorite things with friends and family.

The teddy bears and children's toys in the centerpiece and wreaths are antiques that are displayed in this collector's home year-round as well as during the Christmas season.

To assemble your own treasures, carefully wire each piece to a grapevine or evergreen wreath. Add pinecones or bows to fill in the spaces.

Pressed-Flower Ornaments

Shown on pages 18 and 19.

MATERIALS
A selection of pressable flowers (such as pansy, primula, red geranium, penstemon, phlox, Indian hawthorn, lantana, alyssum, delphinium, queen's wreath, lobelia, verbena, forget-me-not, Queen-Anne's-lace, tansy, honeysuckle, and fern)
Newsprint
Scraps of colored paper or cardboard
Small picture frames (available in crafts stores)
White crafts glue
Clear adhesive vinyl
Narrow ribbon for hanging
Toothpicks
Tweezers
Transparent page protectors

INSTRUCTIONS
TO PRESS FLOWERS AND FOLIAGE: Select newly blossomed flowers (dry, with no dew) and place individual blossoms flat between folded sheets of plain newsprint. Slip these sheets into a botany press (if available) or between the pages of a thick book (a telephone book or encyclopedia, for example). If you use a book, weight it down with heavy objects (bricks or rocks).

(*Note:* A diagram for making a simple flower press appears on page 29.)

Thin-petaled flowers will take six days or less to dry; thick-petaled flowers will take a bit longer. Remove flowers from newsprint and store in transparent page protectors (available in stationery stores).

Do not leave flowers in press or books too long or they will become overly dry and brittle.

Press small ferns and foliage in the same manner. (*Note:* Although most flowers usually keep their colors if dried properly, ferns tend to lose their green color. You may find it necessary to spray each pressed fern with a light coat of flat green paint to give it color.)

MOUNTING THE FLORAL DESIGN: Cut a piece of colored paper or cardboard to match frame (back lightweight paper with cardboard).

Next, select one or two dried and pressed flowers and a few sprigs of greenery to compose your picture. You may want to use one or two larger blossoms and a few sprays of more delicate blossoms to balance the composition.

When the arrangement pleases you, attach each flower, bud, and fern with tiny dabs of white glue (use toothpicks to distribute glue and tweezers to position flowers).

Once pressed flowers are secure and glue is totally dry, frame design as is or protect with a layer of self-adhesive vinyl. Cut adhesive vinyl about ¼ inch larger all around than background. Remove paper backing and carefully apply vinyl over the flower arrangement; press firmly in place and trim away excess vinyl.

To seal, "laminate" vinyl to picture by pressing for a few seconds with a cool iron, using a press cloth. Place laminated picture under a heavy book for a few days so the picture will lie flat. Insert picture in frame and add a loop of ribbon for hanging, if desired.

Potpourri-Filled Glass Balls

Shown on pages 18 and 19.

MATERIALS
Commercial or homemade potpourri
Clear glass Christmas balls
¼-inch-wide satin ribbon (12 inches for each ornament)

INSTRUCTIONS
Purchase commercial potpourri or make your own using the following information. (Allow ½ cup of potpourri for each large glass ball.)

TO MAKE YOUR OWN POTPOURRI: There are dozens of different recipes for potpourri—some for scenting the room, others for freshening the linens, and still others for keeping moths at bay. You may concoct your own special blend of flowers, herbs, and spices by following these simple suggestions.

Floral Potpourri
Some flowers are used in the mixture for their scent (rose and jasmine, for example), and others are included just to add color and texture to the potpourri mix (bachelor's-button and daisy). All of the following flowers dry well and retain a lovely color: rose, marigold, calendula, clematis, bachelor's-button, pansy, peony, aster, nasturtium, zinnia, larkspur, delphinium, sweet alyssum, and dianthus.

Pick the flowers on a dry, sunny day, just before they've reached the height of their bloom. To ensure good ventilation, dry the flower petals on wire screens. Set the screens in a cool, dry, shady place for about two weeks, or until the flower petals are crackly. Also dry a few whole buds and flower heads to add textural interest to your potpourri mix.

For every quart of dried petals, you'll need to add a heaping spoonful of mixed herbs and spices. Favorite herbs include rosemary, mint, lavender, thyme, lemon balm, lemon verbena, and sage. Often-used spices are cloves, cinnamon, cardamom, coriander, nutmeg, mace, allspice, and anise. Most of these herbs and spices are available at natural food stores or herbalist shops.

To preserve the scent of your mixture, you also will need to mix in a large spoonful of fixative. Orrisroot is one that is readily available at pharmacies.

If the mixture's scent is a little too weak, or if you need to "refresh" an aging mixture, add a few drops (no more) of essential oils in one of the following fragrances: rose, lavender, rosemary, rose geranium, honeysuckle, lilac, or bergamot. These oils, too, are available at herbal shops and through a variety of mail-order sources.

Pour the mixture of petals, herbs, spices, and essential oils into an airtight container and set it aside to cure for three to four weeks. Stir the mixture every few days to blend the fragrances and prevent mildew.

Traditional Potpourri
This is a catchall recipe for flowers and herbs that have been collected from a summer garden. Vary ingredients and proportions depending on available materials.

Mix together the following:
3 ounces of rose petals
2 ounces of lavender flowers
1 ounce each of peony, jasmine, chamomile, carnation, and marigold flowers for scent
1 ounce each of lemon balm, marjoram, hyssop, southernwood, rosemary, and meadowsweet, plus ½ ounce each of thyme, peppermint, and crushed bay leaves
Sprinkle in 1 ounce of strawflowers and bachelor's-button for color.

Next, add the following:
4 tablespoons each of cinnamon, allspice, and cloves, plus 1 tablespoon of grated nutmeg
2 ounces each of crushed orange peel and orrisroot
2 drops each of rose, honeysuckle, carnation, lilac, and lavender oils
Cure mixture as described above.

Lavender Sachet Potpourri
This recipe is made entirely from herbs and spices.

Mix together the following:
3 ounces of thyme
½ ounce each of rosemary, wormwood, and melilot
1 ounce of lavender
¼ ounce each of tansy and mint
1 teaspoon each of cloves
 and orrisroot.
Crush all the ingredients together into a fine powder.

TO FILL THE ORNAMENTS: Carefully remove the wire hanger from the top of the glass ball. Hand-fill each ball with ½ cup of potpourri.

Replace the top of the ornament. Thread narrow ribbon through wire hanger and tie in bow for hanger.

Miniature Floral Hats

Shown on page 19.

MATERIALS
Miniature straw hats (available at most crafts stores)
Excelsior or dried Spanish moss (nests)
Dried flowers
Baby's-breath
2 yards of ½-inch-wide satin ribbon
White crafts glue
Newspaper

INSTRUCTIONS
Lay the straw hats on top of old newspaper. Squeeze a band of white crafts glue around the crown of each hat. Arrange small bits of excelsior or moss, dried flowers, and baby's-breath around the crown, pushing the ends into the glue. Allow the glue to dry thoroughly, securing the flowers to the hat.

Cut three 20-inch lengths of narrow ribbon for each hat. Holding the three pieces of ribbon together, tie one bow. Glue the triple bow in place at the back of the brim, on top of the floral band.

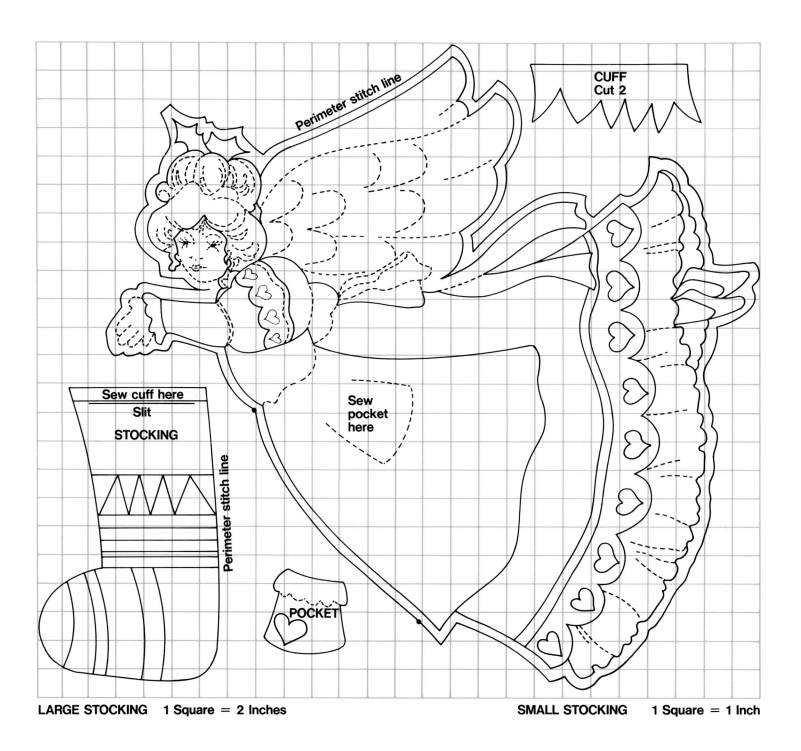

CUFF
Cut 2

Sew cuff here

Slit

STOCKING

Perimeter stitch line

Perimeter stitch line

Sew
pocket
here

POCKET

LARGE STOCKING   1 Square = 2 Inches

SMALL STOCKING   1 Square = 1 Inch

Hearth Angel

Shown on pages 20 and 21.
Finished size is 22x22 inches.

MATERIALS
¾ yard *each* of tear-away pattern paper and muslin
½ yard *each* of white and red fabric
⅛ yard *each* of blue and tan fabric
½ yard of 2-inch-wide muslin ruffling
½ yard of 3-inch-wide ruffled lace
Red, brown, white, and tan thread
Red and brown embroidery thread
Two 24x28-inch pieces of quilt batting
Tracing paper
Six ½-inch-diameter bells

INSTRUCTIONS
Note: The angel and stocking are worked in a type of appliqué. Fabric is not cut out and stitched onto appliquéd areas as in conventional appliqué; instead, a piece of fabric slightly larger than needed is laid over the area to be appliquéd, machine-basted on the background fabric along pattern lines, and then the excess fabric is trimmed away from the outer edge. When all appliqué pieces are basted and trimmed, all raw edges are finished with machine-zigzag stitches.

For the angel
Enlarge the pattern, *opposite,* onto tracing paper.

PREPARING THE APPLIQUÉ: Place tear-away pattern paper over the enlarged pattern; trace the design onto pattern paper with a pencil. Lay muslin on a work surface. With drawing side up, pin the pattern paper to muslin. Sewing on the pattern paper side and following the drawn line with straight stitches, machine-stitch pieces together along the perimeter line.

Note: The muslin side is the right side. Continue to work on the pattern paper side (wrong side) using the drawn lines as stitching lines.

Lay white fabric right side down under the apron area; center the angel (drawing side up) on white fabric and pin in several places. With straight stitches, machine-stitch along each line (solid and dotted) of the apron and ties.

Turn the angel over and cut away excess fabric around outer edges of the white shapes, cutting close to the stitching line.

Repeat procedure for tan dress, blue ruffle, and red trim. Repeat for the brown hair and tan wings.

Appliqué hearts on the sleeve and dress ruffle (see pattern). Cut away skirt ruffle along scallops and finish it with zigzag stitches. Cut a separate muslin piece for the remaining part of the skirt to place behind the scallops (draw around the pattern from the red stripe). Sew behind the scalloped edge under the red stripe edge. Sew muslin ruffling under the scalloped edge. Sew a lace ruffle ¾ inch away from the muslin ruffling.

On the wrong side, machine-stitch hair and face detail with tiny straight stitches.

Zigzag the raw edge of the pocket top to finish. Zigzag the pocket to the apron, leaving the top open.

APPLIQUÉ: With your machine set at a ⅛-inch-wide zigzag satin stitch, machine-appliqué over all straight-stitched lines with matching threads on right side of angel, *except* hair and face. For face, use narrow zigzag stitch lines over all lines. Fill in mouth with wider stitches, adjusting width on machine as you sew. For hair, use ⅛-inch-wide zigzag stitches to outline main hair shapes (refer to photograph on page 21).

FINISHING: Tear away all pattern paper, *except* behind the face and hands. Lay two 24x28-inch layers of quilt batting on a work surface, cover batting with muslin, and lay the angel over the muslin right side down; pin layers together. Stitch together along the perimeter line, leaving an opening for turning between dots; clip seams, turn, and push corners out. Press and sew closed. Machine- or hand-quilt with long straight stitches along the dress back and around the apron. Add a thread hanger to back.

For the stocking
Appliqué the stocking front as for the angel front above, *except* use red fabric instead of muslin. Add patches of tan and green fabric over the red fabric.

Sew a row of zigzag stitches on each side of the slit (stocking opening). Like a giant buttonhole, slit the stocking top open.

For the cuff, lay two layers of fabric, right sides facing, onto tear-away pattern piece. Straight-stitch around points stopping and starting at dots. Remove tear-away pattern paper, clip seams, and turn cuff. Trim top; place the cuff top along the bottom of the slit on stocking front and satin-stitch together.

To finish, cover the stocking front with muslin and sew around perimeter line (be sure cuff points are tucked away from seam line). Clip the seams and turn the stocking right side out through the slit. Sew bells at the ends of the points. Hand-sew the stocking to the angel's hand.

COLOR KEY

	DMC	Bates
Dk. Brown	898	0360
Dk. Rose	3350	069
Pink	3354	074
Med. Gray	927	975
Steel Blue	930	978

1234567890

Deborah Collins-1989

A B C D E F G H I J
K L M N O P Q R
S T U V W X Y Z

a b c d e f g h i j k l m
n o p q r s t u v w x y z

Patchwork Stocking

Shown on page 20.
Finished size is 20 inches tall.

MATERIALS
½ yard *each* of tear-away pattern
  paper and red calico
¼ yard (total) of green calico scraps
⅛ yard of tan calico
Red and green sewing thread
Six ¾-inch-diameter jingle bells

INSTRUCTIONS
Follow the instructions given for the
angel stocking on page 27, except
enlarge the pattern to a scale of 1
square = 2 inches.

Joy Hanging

Shown on page 20.
Finished size is 11x15 inches.

MATERIALS
5 feet of ¾-inch-diameter paper
  core
⅓ yard of brick-red fabric
Red thread
Two coat hangers
Masking tape

INSTRUCTIONS
On paper, draw the JOY letters.
Straighten out coat-hanger wires
and shape them like the letter you
have drawn. With tape, fasten paper
core to the coat-hanger letters.
  Tear fabric into 1½-inch-wide
strips. Wrap each letter to cover once
or twice. Using fabric strips, tie the
letters together. Secure the ends
with thread.

Patchwork Sampler

Shown on page 20.
Finished size is 15¾x20¾ inches.

MATERIALS
23x26-inch piece of white
  hardanger fabric
Embroidery floss in the following
  colors and amounts: Three
  skeins of blue; two skeins *each*
  of medium gray, pink, and dark
  rose; one skein of dark brown
Embroidery needle
Embroidery hoop

INSTRUCTIONS
Chart pattern, *opposite,* onto graph
paper, or stitch from our chart.
  Find the center of the design and
the center of the fabric; begin stitching here. Thread the needle with two
strands of embroidery floss and
stitch the cross-stitches over two
threads of fabric. Use two strands of
floss for outlining each quilt design
and the sampler center design. (This
outline is indicated by the dotted line
on the pattern.)
  Press the finished sampler on the
back side; frame as desired.

Rag Heart

Shown on page 20.

MATERIALS
Plastic-foam heart (8½ inches
  across at the widest point)
½ yard of brick-red fabric

INSTRUCTIONS
Tear fabric into 1½-inch-wide strips.
Wrap foam heart with fabric strips
to cover. Tear remaining strips into
12-inch lengths. Loop strips around
heart and knot close to the form,
leaving ends free.

MAKING A FLOWER PRESS

1. Tape two 8-inch squares
   of plywood together.

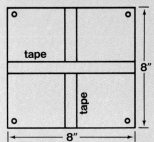

■ Measure ½ inch in from each
  edge and drill a ¼-inch hole
  through each corner. Remove
  the tape.

2. Cut cardboard, felt, and unprinted
   newsprint into 8-inch squares.

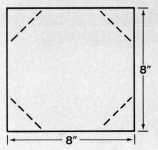

■ Trim off all corners at
  45-degree angles.

3. Place a ¼-inch flat washer on
   a carriage bolt. Push it up through
   the bottom piece of plywood.

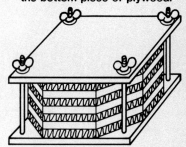

■ Fill the press.

■ Top with the second piece
  of plywood. Slip a washer
  over the end of each bolt.
  Tighten with a wing nut.

A COZY LOG CABIN CHRISTMAS

If walls could speak of holidays past, this log cabin would have wondrous stories to tell. And yet, the memories being made today are no doubt among the happiest.

The character and charm of this authentic cabin can only be matched by that of its owner. Her tremendous love for the state of Tennessee and its people are quickly evident in her display of handcrafted treasures, old and new. Friends from far and near add to her collection with each visit. Gift-wrapped in country Christmas colors, the cabin shown here and on the following pages is bursting with holiday trimmings for you to make. The LeMoyne Star quilt and Spiderweb bed pillow are antique pieces that you can reproduce with scraps of red and green calico.

Muslin and canvas Santas and stockings, string-pieced pillows and table covering, and a host of homespun tree ornaments will give your country "cabin" this same enchantment. (Turn the page to take a closer look.)

Instructions for projects follow on page 36.

Scraps of muslin, a bit of paint, and a strong batch of tea for aging are the main ingredients for the old-fashioned Santas, *right* and *opposite.* Primitive in design, yet absolutely charming, each one can be made as simple or as elaborate as you like. Fabric appliqué, embroidery stitches, and clothing embellishments give each of the Santas its own unique personality. The purchased lampshade, *right,* and the gift bag, *opposite,* share the same Saint Nick stencil motif. Use the design on tree ornaments (page 35), wrapping paper, greeting cards, and other gifts to set the scene for a jolly country Christmas.

A COZY LOG CABIN CHRISTMAS

For a great way to use fabric scraps, string-piece a wall hanging and octagon-shaped pillow like those, *opposite*. Cut the fabrics into thin strips, sew them together, and make a variety of festive accessories.

Cut the angel tree-topper, *left*, from pine.

Sand smooth, and paint her in your favorite country colors.

Craft old-world Santas and stockings, *below*, from canvas stiffened with gesso and acrylic paint. Fill the 22-inch-long stockings to the toe with sweets and surprises.

LeMoyne Star Quilt

Shown on pages 30 and 31.
Finished quilt is 71½x84 inches.
Finished block is 12½x12½ inches.

MATERIALS
(All yardages are for 44- to 45-inch-
    wide fabric.)

4¼ yards of green print fabric
Approximately 1¾ yards of
    assorted white print fabric scraps
Approximately 1¾ yards of
    assorted pink, red, and black
    print fabric scraps
5 yards of fabric for quilt back
Quilt batting
Cardboard or plastic for templates
Graph paper

INSTRUCTIONS
Cutting directions for borders include ¼-inch seam allowances. Template patterns are finished size; add
¼-inch seam allowances when cutting these pieces from fabrics. Sew
all pieces with right sides facing, taking ¼-inch seams.

TO BEGIN: Make cardboard or plastic templates for the patterns, *below.*
Draw around templates with a pencil on the wrong sides of the fabrics;
cut out the pieces, adding ¼-inch
seam allowances.

FABRIC CUTTING INSTRUCTIONS:
From the green print fabric, cut four
5x78-inch borders. (Borders are cut
longer than needed and are trimmed
to length when added to the quilt
top.) Adding ¼-inch seam allowances, cut 120 B triangles with the
long side of the triangle on the fabric
grain; cut 120 C squares.
  Adding seam allowances, cut 120
A diamonds from the white print
fabrics. Cut 120 A diamonds from

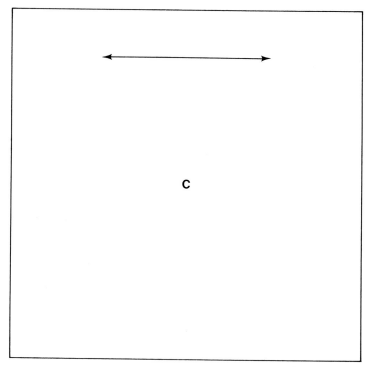

A

B

C

LEMOYNE STAR QUILT

Full-Size Patterns

the red and pink print fabrics. Each star block requires two sets of four matching diamonds (four white and four dark).

BLOCK PIECING INSTRUCTIONS: Join eight A diamonds into a star, alternating white and dark diamonds. Set a B triangle into every other opening around the star.

Set a C square into the remaining four openings.

Make 30 LeMoyne Star blocks.

QUILT TOP INSTRUCTIONS: Sew blocks in six horizontal rows with five blocks in each row; join the rows. Sew a border to opposite long sides of quilt; trim borders even with the quilt. Sew the remaining borders to the quilt top and bottom; trim.

FINISHING INSTRUCTIONS: To piece the quilt back, cut the backing fabric into two 2½-yard panels. Split one panel in half lengthwise. Taking ½-inch seam allowances and match-ing selvage edges, sew a half-panel to each side of the full panel. Trim seam allowances to approximately ¼ inch. Press seams to one side. Lay-er the quilt top, batting, and back-ing; baste. Quilt as desired.

When quilting is complete, trim the quilt back and batting even with the top. Turn fabric in ¼ inch on both the quilt top and quilt back.

Trim batting again so it is slightly smaller than the folded edges. To fin-ish the outer edges, stitch the folded edges of quilt top and back together, concealing the batting.

STENCILED SANTA BAG AND ORNAMENT
Full-Size Stencils:

A
B
C

Ornament Outline

Open

Stenciled Bag, Lampshade, And Ornament

Shown on pages 32, 33, and 35. Finished sizes are 3½x4½ inches (ornaments) and 8½x10 inches (bag).

MATERIALS
Tissue paper
Stencil brush
Stencil plastic
Stencil cutting knife
Acrylic stencil paint in red, white, and flesh colors
Black fine-tip permanent marker
Even-weave fabric in ecru or tan
Twine
Scraps of cotton fabric (for ornament backing)
Polyester fiberfill

INSTRUCTIONS
CUTTING THE STENCIL: Trace the full-size Santa stencil pattern, *left,* and the holly pattern on page 38 onto tissue paper. Cut one plastic pattern for *each* color used on the stencil design and use a piece of plas-tic large enough to encompass the entire pattern, plus a 1-inch margin.
continued

37

STENCILED HOLLY
Full-Size Stencil

Cut one stencil for the beard, mustache, and white trim on the hat; one for the top of the hat; and one for the face area. Cut one stencil for the holly used on the bag and the lampshade. (Do not cut out the berries.)

For the bag
Cut a piece of even-weave fabric 9¼x24 inches; fold it in half so that it measures 9¼x12 inches.

With right sides facing, stitch along each side. Hem the top edge so when the bag is turned, the hem faces the inside. Turn the bag right side out and press it flat.

Stenciling one color at a time and allowing each color to dry before continuing to the next, stencil Santa and holly leaves on the bag. Add the berries with the tip of a paintbrush. Outline Santa shape with black marker. Add the eye with a marker.

Fill bag and tie top with twine.

For the lampshade
Stencil designs on purchased lampshade, following instructions *above.*

For the ornament
The egg-shaped outline around the Santa pattern on page 37 is full-size for the finished ornament. Add ¼-inch seam allowances before cutting. Cut one even-weave fabric front and one cotton backing.

Stencil the Santa design on the front fabric piece of each ornament.

With right sides facing, stitch the front to the back. Leave an opening

at the bottom for turning. Turn right side out; stuff; stitch opening closed.

Hand-stitch a length of twine to the top for tying ornament to tree.

Muslin Santas

Shown on pages 30–33.
Finished sizes range from 9½ to 13 inches tall.

MATERIALS
Scraps of muslin
Scraps of red fabric
Twine (for belt)
Black acrylic paint or permanent marker for outlining
Acrylic paint in red, white, gold, and green
Instant tea
Artist's brushes
Sawdust
Quilting thread
Sewing needle

INSTRUCTIONS
Note: Instructions are for painting muslin Santas. You may combine painting, appliqué, embroidery, and quilting to create your own designs.

PAINTING THE SANTAS: The pattern, *right* and *opposite,* is full size for the Santa in the photo on page 32. Join the pattern at the AB lines as marked before cutting. Vary the size and body shape, and make an entire collection of dolls.

Transfer the pattern to tissue paper. Cut out shape. Draw around the outline on muslin. Transfer the clothing and facial details to fabric. Do not cut out.

Outline all details with permanent black marking pen. Use an artist's brush and tea to dye the face area.

Thin acrylics before painting beard and clothing. Dip brush into the paint, dab the brush on paper

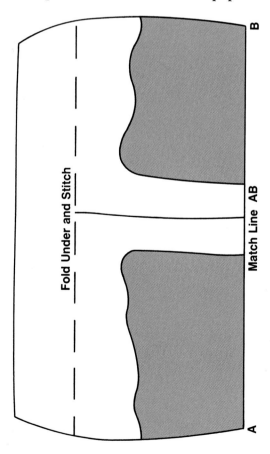

towels to remove excess, and lightly brush a hint of color on clothing, beard, hands, belt, etc. (Refer to the photographs on pages 32 and 33.)

TO STITCH THE SANTA: With right sides facing, lay the painted Santa front atop a second piece of muslin. Using the outline of the front as a sewing guide, stitch the front and back pieces of muslin together. Leave the bottom edge unstitched. Cut out shape ¼ inch outside of the seam line. Turn right side out. Stuff firmly with sawdust. Overlap the bottom edges and stitch closed with a needle and quilting thread. Tap the bottom edge on a hard surface to create a flat, solid bottom surface.

String Star Pillows

The square pillow is shown on page 31; the octagon pillow is shown on page 34.
Finished pillows are 18x18 inches, excluding ruffles.

MATERIALS
For two pillows
2 yards of plaid fabric
1 yard of olive green print fabric
1 yard of muslin
1 yard total of assorted red, green, and tan print fabric scraps
Two 20-inch squares of quilt batting or polyester fleece
Graph paper
Plastic or cardboard for templates
Plastic-coated freezer paper
Polyester fiberfill

INSTRUCTIONS
TO MAKE THE PATTERNS: Draw two 4¾-inch squares onto graph paper. Divide one square in half into two triangles. From cardboard or plastic, make a template for the square, for the triangle, and for the diamond pattern on page 40. Transfer the arrow on the diamond pattern to the diamond template. All patterns are finished size; add ¼-inch seam allowances when cutting pieces from fabric.

continued

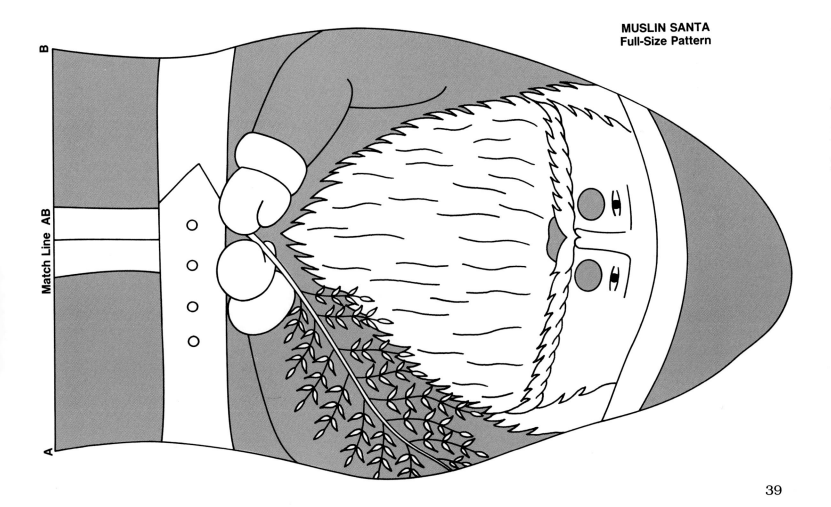

MUSLIN SANTA
Full-Size Pattern

B

Match Line AB

A

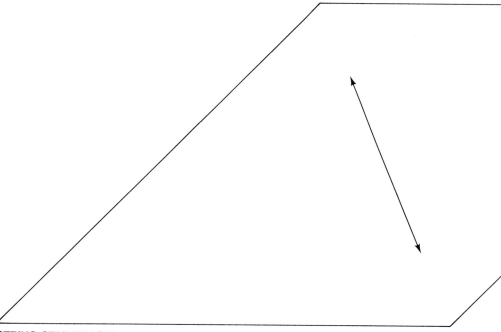

STRING STAR PILLOW　　　　　　　　　　　　**Full-Size Pattern**

TO CUT THE FABRICS: From the muslin, cut two 20-inch squares for the pillow linings.

From the olive print fabric, cut two 20-inch squares for the pillow backs. Cut four 1½x45-inch strips across the fabric width for the trim.

From the assorted print fabric scraps, cut a variety of 45-inch-long strips across the fabric width ranging from ½ to 1¾ inches wide.

TO MAKE THE DIAMONDS: Using the diamond template, cut 16 diamonds from the freezer paper. Transfer the arrow to each diamond. Cut out the paper diamonds; do not add seam allowances.

Join strips, lengthwise, into two rectangles that are 10 or more inches wide. Sew fabric strips in random sequence and a pleasing arrangement of colors. Press seam allowances to one side.

Position eight paper diamonds, coating side down, onto the wrong side of a pieced fabric rectangle. Place the diamonds with the arrow along a seam or other consistent position. Space diamonds to allow for ¼-inch seam allowance around diamonds. With a warm dry iron, press diamonds onto fabric. Cut out diamonds, adding seam allowances. Repeat to cut eight diamonds from the other set of pieced fabric strips.

Choose eight diamonds for each star (four diamonds from each fabric combination). Join pairs of diamonds, sewing along the edge of the paper. (Do not sew beyond the paper. Leave the fabric seam allowance unsewn at each end of the seam.) Backstitch at the beginning and end of the seams. Join the pairs of diamonds into half-stars. Join the halves to form stars.

For the square pillow
From muslin, cut four squares, using the square template. Using the triangle template, cut four triangles with the long side on the fabric grain (see arrow on pattern).

Set the four triangles into alternate openings around the outside of the star. Set the four squares into the remaining openings.

Cut two of the olive print trim strips in half into strips approximately 22 inches long. Sew a strip onto opposite sides of the star; trim strips even with the edge. Sew the remaining strips onto the other two sides and trim.

Layer and baste the muslin lining square, quilt batting, and the star block. Quilt "in the ditch," along all seam lines, by either hand or machine. Baste around the outer edge of the block and trim excess batting and lining.

From the red plaid fabric, cut approximately 160 inches of 6½-inch-wide bias strips for the ruffle. Join bias strips into a loop. Press the ruffle in half, wrong sides together, so that the ruffle is 3¼ inches wide. Divide ruffle into fourths. Gather one-fourth of the ruffle onto each side of the pillow; baste. Stitch pillow top to pillow back, leaving an opening for turning. Turn, stuff, and stitch opening closed.

For the octagonal pillow

From muslin, use the triangle template to cut eight triangles with the long side on the fabric grain.

Set a triangle into each opening around the star.

Cut two olive trim strips into eight strips, each approximately 10 inches long. Sew a strip to alternate triangles around the star; press. Sew the remaining strips to the remaining triangles. Trim excess strips, forming an octagon.

Finish the octagonal pillow as directed for the square pillow, *opposite*, except divide the ruffle into eight sections rather than four.

Spiderweb Pillow

Shown on pages 30–31, and 34. Finished size of pillow, excluding the ruffle, is 17 inches square.

MATERIALS

1½ yards of green stripe fabric
½ yard of red stripe fabric
¼ yard each of muslin and dark
   green print fabric
2¼ yards of yellow piping
Cardboard or plastic for templates
Polyester fiberfill

INSTRUCTIONS

The patterns are finished size; add ¼-inch seam allowances when cutting pieces from fabric. The dimensions for the other pieces include seam allowances. Sew all pieces with right sides facing, taking ¼-inch seams unless otherwise directed.

CUTTING INSTRUCTIONS: Trace and make cardboard or plastic templates for patterns, *right*. To cut patchwork pieces, draw around template with a pencil on the wrong side of the fabric; cut out the pieces, adding ¼-inch seam allowances.

continued

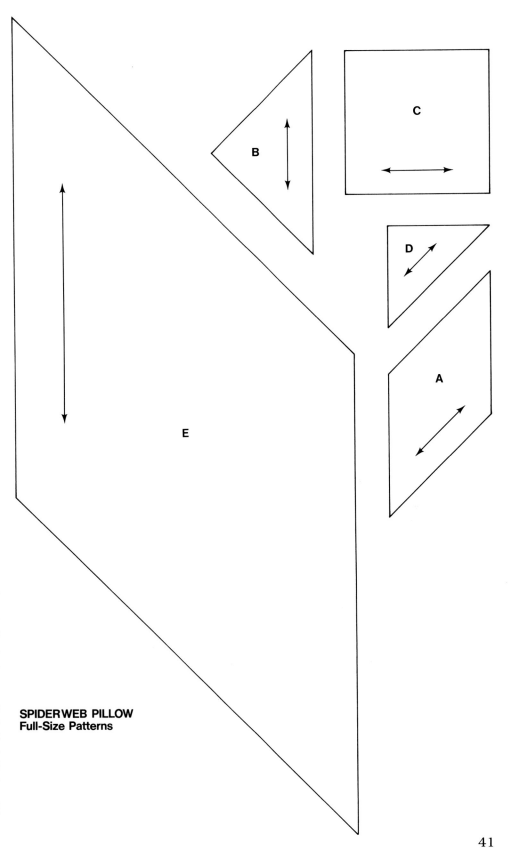

SPIDERWEB PILLOW
Full-Size Patterns

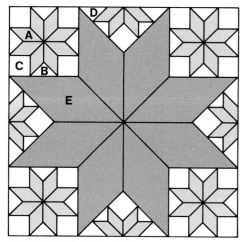

SPIDERWEB STAR DIAGRAM

From the red stripe fabric, cut eight E diamonds.

From the green fabric, cut 48 A diamonds.

From the muslin, cut 24 B triangles and eight D triangles with the long side of the triangles on the fabric grain. Cut 20 C squares.

TO MAKE THE SMALL STARS: Referring to the diagram, *above,* join eight A diamonds to form a star. Set a B triangle into alternate openings between diamonds around the star. Set a C square into the remaining openings to complete a star. Make four stars.

To make a half-star, join four A diamonds. Set a C square into the opening between the middle two diamonds. Set a B triangle into the openings to the sides of the square. Sew a D triangle to the side of each of the outer diamonds to complete a half-star. Make four half-stars.

TO MAKE THE BLOCK: Join eight E diamonds into a star. Set a small star into alternate openings between diamonds around the outside of the star. Set a half-star into the remaining openings to complete the block.

FINISHING THE PILLOW: Baste the piping around the pillow along the seam line.

For the pillow back, cut a 17½-inch square from the green stripe fabric. From the remaining green stripe fabric, cut 7½-inch-wide bias strips for the pillow ruffle. Piece the strips together into a loop that measures approximately 3½ yards in circumference. Press the ruffle in half, wrong sides together and raw edges even. Run gathering threads ¼ inch from the raw edge of the ruffle. Divide the ruffle into fourths. Gather one-fourth of the ruffle to each side of the pillow top. Sew the ruffle atop the piping.

Sew the pillow top to the back, right sides together; leave an opening for turning. Clip corners, turn, stuff, and sew the opening closed.

String-Pieced Christmas Coverlet

Shown on pages 30–31 (on table), and 34 (hanging on wall).
Finished coverlet measures approximately 65½x73½ inches.

MATERIALS

1⅞ yards green print fabric for setting strips
Scraps of assorted red, green, and tan print fabrics for patchwork
4½ yards green print fabric for quilt back and binding
Quilt batting
Roll of 18-inch-wide shelf paper

INSTRUCTIONS
Note: All cutting measurements include ¼-inch seam allowances.

CUTTING THE PIECES: From the green setting strip fabric, cut three strips, *each* 4x63 inches; two strips, *each* 6x63 inches; and two strips, *each* 6x65½ inches.

STRING-PIECED COVERLET DIAGRAM

From the shelf paper, cut four pieces, *each* 9x63 inches, to use as the foundation for the patchwork. Mark placement lines for the patchwork on the paper pieces. On two paper strips, mark a dot 31½ inches from the top along the left edge of the paper. On the same paper pieces, mark a dot 40½ inches from the top along the right edge. Using a ruler, connect the dots to draw a line at a 45-degree angle on the paper pieces. Mark the other two paper pieces so the placement lines angle in the opposite direction.

From the assorted print fabric scraps and the remaining green setting strip fabric, cut strips for patchwork across the fabric width. From each fabric, cut strips in widths ranging from 1 to 3 inches wide.

TO PIECE THE STRIPS: Pin two different fabric strips right sides together along the placement line on a paper piece. Position the fabric strips so that when they are opened out the paper will be covered by the fabric. Set the stitch length on your sewing machine at approximately 15–20 stitches per inch. Taking ¼-inch seams, sew along one side of the strips, stitching through the paper. Open the fabric strips and press the seam open. Trim excess fabric even with the paper.

Choose another fabric strip and pin it, right sides together, along one of the previously sewn strips. Stitch the strip, press, and trim even with the paper. In the same manner, add strips of various colors and widths until the paper is covered with patchwork. Turn the strip over and tear off the paper from the wrong side. Tear carefully, being careful not to loosen the stitching along the edges. Work patchwork on the remaining paper pieces.

Alternating the slant of the patchwork, sew the patchwork strips together with 4-inch-wide setting strips between the patchwork strips. Sew 6x63-inch setting strips to opposite sides. Sew the 6x65½-inch setting strips to the top and bottom of the quilt top.

TO PIECE THE QUILT BACK: Cut the quilt back fabric into two equal lengths. Trim one panel to measure 28 inches wide. Matching selvages, sew the two panels together, taking a ½-inch seam. Press seam allowance to one side and trim seam allowance to ¼ inch.

TO FINISH THE QUILT: Layer the back, batting, and quilt top; baste. Hand- or machine-quilt as desired.

When quilting is complete, trim the quilt back so it is 1 inch larger than the quilt top on all sides. Trim the batting so it is ½ inch larger than the quilt top on all sides. Fold the quilt back over to cover the batting; fold quilt back over onto quilt top to cover the raw edge. Hand- or machine-stitch the folded edge of the quilt back to the quilt top.

Old-World Santas And Stockings

Shown on page 35.
Finished stocking is 22 inches long and Santa is 8 inches tall.

MATERIALS
Canvas
Gesso primer
Acrylic paint in green, red, black, brown, white, and flesh-tone
Antiquing glaze
Polyester fiberfill
Plastic bags
Leather shoelace

INSTRUCTIONS
For the stocking
Enlarge the pattern, *below,* onto paper. Transfer the pattern to canvas. Cut out two stocking shapes and one stocking cuff.

With right sides facing, sew the two stocking shapes together. Leave the top open. Clip all curves; turn the stocking right side out.

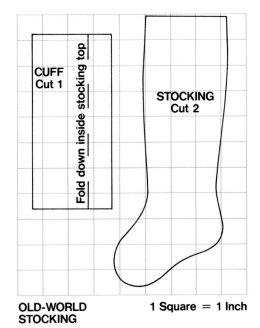

CUFF
Cut 1

Fold down inside stocking top

STOCKING
Cut 2

OLD-WORLD STOCKING   1 Square = 1 Inch

Stuff the inside of the stocking with plastic bags to give it the desired shape. If you are making more than one stocking, vary the shape of each to make them more interesting when displayed. (*Note:* The plastic bags will be removed when the stocking is finished.)

Coat the entire stocking shape with gesso. Allow it to dry for 24 hours. If the shape does not feel stiff, apply a second coat. Allow another 24 hours for drying.

Apply several coats of acrylic paint in red or green. Allow each coat of paint to dry thoroughly before going to the next.

TO ADD THE CUFF: Machine-hem the bottom and two sides of the cuff. Fold the cuff as marked by the line of dashes on the pattern. Tuck the top edge inside of the stocking top. Glue the cuff in place.

Poke a hole through the back top edge of the stocking. Tie a 5-inch length of leather shoelace through the hole, forming a loop for hanging. Prepare and paint the cuff and leather loop exactly the way you did the body of the stocking.

TO FINISH THE STOCKING: Apply the antiquing glaze to the entire stocking, including the cuff and leather loop. Wipe off excess glaze to allow the color to show through. Allow the glaze to dry thoroughly. Finish with one coat of clear varnish. Dry thoroughly.

For the Santa
Enlarge the pattern on page 44 onto paper. Transfer to canvas.

Cut two Santa shapes. With right sides facing, sew the two shapes together. Leave the bottom open for turning. Turn right side out. Stuff with polyester fiberfill. Overlap the
continued

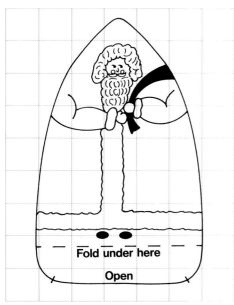

OLD-WORLD SANTA   **1 Square = 1 Inch**

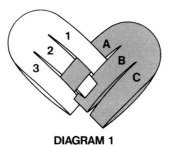

DIAGRAM 1

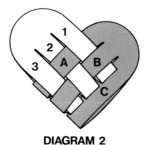

DIAGRAM 2

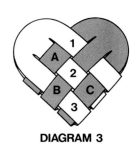

DIAGRAM 3

Paper Heart Ornaments

Shown on pages 31 and 35.
Finished size is 4x4 inches.

MATERIALS
Pretwisted craft paper in red and
  brown
Tissue paper
Large-eye needle
Twine
Baby's-breath

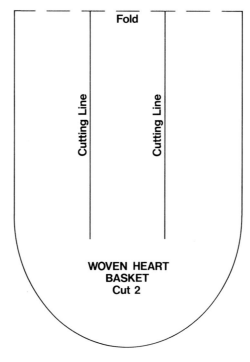

Fold

Cutting Line

Cutting Line

**WOVEN HEART
BASKET
Cut 2**

INSTRUCTIONS
The pattern, *below,* is full size. Trace
the pattern onto folded tissue paper;
cut out and unfold the tissue.

Untwist a length of pretwisted paper. Cut one pattern from red paper
and one from brown paper.

Fold the paper pieces in half and
cut slits through the middle as
marked on the pattern. Weave two
shapes together to form the heart,
following the diagrams, *above.*

Cut brown paper into a 14-inch
length; untwist. Cut in half lengthwise. Cut each half into three equal
strips and braid. Tie a knot at each
end. Hand-stitch the braided handle
to the heart ornament using large-
eye needle and twine. Tuck baby's-
breath or any dried flowers inside of
finished paper heart.

Painted Angel

Shown on page 35.
Finished size is 8¾ inches high x 15
inches long.

MATERIALS
17-inch length of 1x12-inch fir or
  pine
Light tan (flesh), dark green, light
  green, black, white, and metallic
  gold acrylic paints
Brown iron oxide acrylic paint
Red iron oxide acrylic paint
Water-base clear varnish
Antiquing glaze
Soft cloth
Sawtooth metal hanging

bottom edges so that the finished
Santa will sit upright.

Apply a coat of gesso to the Santa
shape. As the gesso dries, push
downward on the shape to flatten
the bottom. Allow the gesso to dry for
24 hours. Apply a second coat to add
stiffness. Dry thoroughly.

Paint the entire Santa shape with
red acrylic paint. Flatten the bottom
of the shape each time you paint.

Paint the face flesh color, the eyes
and nose black, and the cheeks red.
Paint the shoes, hands, and the outline of the arms black. Use white
acrylic to paint the cuffs and fur
down the front of Santa's suit. Load
the brush heavily with white acrylic
paint, and paint the hair and beard
in C-swirls to imitate curls.

The hands are positioned to hold a
bag. Paint a black bag shape up and
over the shoulder and onto the back
of the shape. Allow each color to dry
thoroughly.

TO FINISH THE SANTA: Apply the
antiquing glaze to the entire Santa.
Allow the glaze to dry thoroughly.
Finish with one coat of clear varnish.
Dry thoroughly.

PAINTED ANGEL

1 Square = 1 Inch

INSTRUCTIONS

Enlarge and transfer the pattern, *above*, onto graph paper. Transfer the pattern to wood; cut out the angel shape.

Note: It is important to allow each color of paint to dry before continuing with the next color.

Paint the angel's face area with acrylic flesh-tone paint. Shade under the chin area with brown iron oxide. Mix red iron oxide with flesh-tone acrylic to make a nice color for the cheeks. Add a little more red iron oxide to the cheek paint mixture to get the rose color for the mouth.

Paint the eye area white. On top of the white, paint the eye dark green.

Paint the pupil black; add a tiny white dot on the upper right-hand corner for a highlight. Line the eyes and eyebrows with dark brown. Paint the halo metallic gold.

Fill in the gown area with dark green. Add a touch of black to the green paint for shading around the sleeve and the folds in the gown and sleeve area.

Paint the trim on the gown light green. Outline the band of light green and the swirls on the band in metallic gold. Paint the collar white.

To shade the wing, load the brush heavily with white. Paint several thick strokes, leaving paint in the ridges for a feathered look.

The hair is painted in the same manner as the wing, but with a smaller round brush. The color is light and dark brown, mixed with a touch of black for contrast.

Paint the heart with red iron oxide; add the swirls with gold.

Paint the hand with flesh-tone, and shade the fingers with brown iron oxide. Paint the slippers black.

Seal the finished painting with water-base varnish. Three coats are recommended, with ample drying time between coats.

Brush antiquing glaze over the entire angel, including the sides. Wipe off the glaze, leaving the glaze lighter in the middle and darker on the edges. Allow the glaze to dry. Apply a final coat of varnish. Dry thoroughly.

HOLIDAY
SAMPLERS

*As warm and inviting as
the homespun quilt and old pine
cupboard, these cross-stitch
greetings summon guests to share in
the joy of Christmas in the country.*

The charming, yet simple, design of the trio of samplers, *opposite,* reminds us of the pioneer women's need to create beauty from scraps.

Bits of fabric and floss are combined with satin bows and silver star appliqués against red, white, and blue Aida cloth backgrounds.

French knots, long stitches, and backstitches add the variety that makes handcrafting so

enjoyable. When stitches are sewn on a richly colored background, patterns often look more intricate than they are.

Designed for quick and easy workup, each project can be completed in a weekend. For last-minute gifts that will look as if they took months of planning, cross-stitch one or all of these holiday greetings.

Instructions and patterns follow on pages 48 and 49.

Holiday Samplers

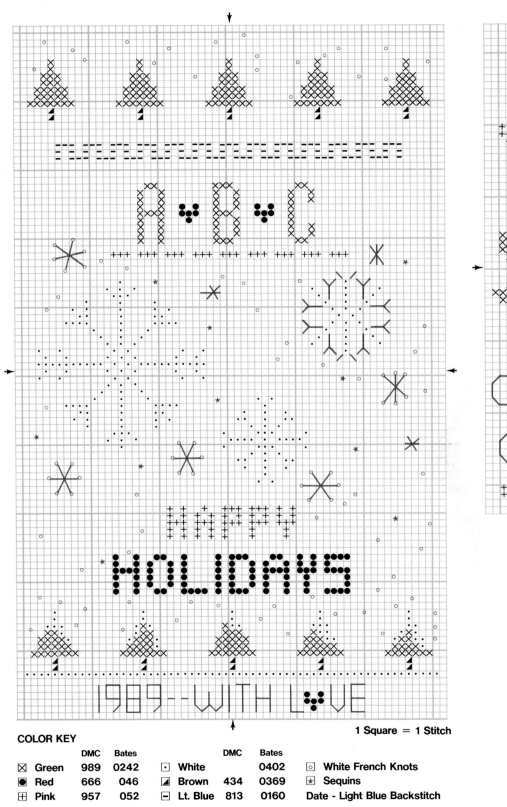

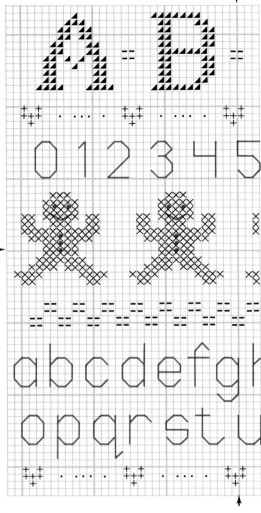

1 Square = 1 Stitch

COLOR KEY

		DMC	Bates
⊡	Blue	797	0147
⊠	Brown	433	0371
⊞	Pink	962	052

Numbers - Green Backstitch

COLOR KEY

		DMC	Bates				DMC	Bates			
⊠	Green	989	0242	⊡	White		0402	⊙	White French Knots
⬤	Red	666	046	◪	Brown	434	0369	✸	Sequins
⊞	Pink	957	052	⊟	Lt. Blue	813	0160		**Date - Light Blue Backstitch**

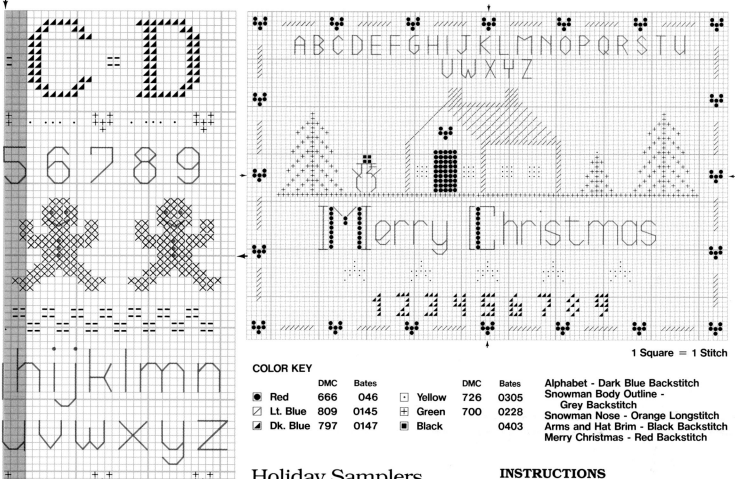

1 Square = 1 Stitch

COLOR KEY

		DMC	Bates			DMC	Bates
●	Red	666	046	⊡	Yellow	726	0305
⬕	Lt. Blue	809	0145	⊞	Green	700	0228
◪	Dk. Blue	797	0147	■	Black		0403

Alphabet - Dark Blue Backstitch
Snowman Body Outline -
   Grey Backstitch
Snowman Nose - Orange Longstitch
Arms and Hat Brim - Black Backstitch
Merry Christmas - Red Backstitch

1 Square = 1 Stitch

COLOR KEY

		DMC	Bates
⊡	White		0402
⊟	Yellow	743	0302
☐	Green	701	0227

Alphabet - Blue Backstitch

Holiday Samplers

Shown on pages 46 and 47.
Finished sizes are 6x6½ inches
(*left*), 6x9½ inches (*center*), 6½x9½
inches (*right*). Sizes exclude frames.

MATERIALS
For one sampler
12-count Aida cloth measuring 2
  inches larger on all sides than
  the finished cross-stitch
Embroidery floss in colors listed on
  color key
⅛-inch satin ribbon (for
  gingerbread men)
Silver star sequin appliqués (for
  snowflakes)

INSTRUCTIONS
(*Note:* The shaded stitches on the
portion of the pattern on page 49 indicate where the pattern on page 48
overlaps. *Do not repeat these stitch-*
es.) Separate the embroidery floss
and use three strands to work the
cross-stitches.

Stitch each counted cross-stitch
over one thread of Aida fabric.

Note: Solid lines on the patterns
indicate areas of long stitches and
backstitches.

Tack tiny satin bows to the neckline of the gingerbread men. Refer to
the photograph on pages 46 and 47.

Sew tiny silver star appliqués
among the snowflakes of the sampler in the center of the photograph.
Frame as desired.

A HEARTY INVITATION TO THE FARM

As crisp and refreshing as the country air, this collection of down-on-the-farm decorations and gifts invites all to enjoy a homespun holiday on the farm.

Hospitality is the heart of Christmas in the country, and this dining room is ever-ready for no-fuss entertaining.

These heart-shaped place mats, *right,* are stitched from prequilted muslin, then dyed a delicate shade of tan. Colorfully stenciled borders, hearts, houses, and the words "Home Sweet Home" complete the mats.

The simple materials of home and farm are all you need to create these primitive reindeer and pine trees. Use a saber saw to cut the wooden figures from pine, then color the deer with acrylic paints. Twig antlers and ribbon neckties finish the woodland trio.

Instructions and patterns for all projects begin on page 56.

50

Greet all who come to call with the delightful barnyard wreath, *left.* To make this whimsical door decoration, wrap sphagnum moss around a plastic foam wreath. Cut the farmer, barn, and animals from pine with a band saw. Paint the figures with acrylics, and attach them to the wreath with floral picks and glue.

A friendly farm scene is found on the 22x34-inch geese and cow hooked rug, *above*. This charming piece of folk art is worked in the traditional manner with strips of wool fabric on a burlap backing.

A striking complement to the hooked rug, the 12-inch needlepoint calico cat, *above*, can be stitched for a pillow or soft toy. Or, fill in the background with white wool yarn and frame the feline portrait.

Stockings, *right*, are fashioned from a well-worn crazy quilt and call to mind the country adage "waste not, want not." If you have any quilt that is worn beyond repair, put it to good use for your family stockings. Add touches of embroidery and old lace for embellishments.

A HEARTY INVITATION TO THE FARM

No matter how far from home they may have roamed, when the Christmas season rolls around, young and old alike look forward to sharing special times with family and friends. When your loved ones gather for the holiday festivities, be prepared to celebrate with good, old-fashioned fun.

A game table is a great gift that the entire family will enjoy. And when it is adorned with folk art motifs like this one, *left*, it is sure to become an heirloom, treasured for generations to come.

To make this stenciled beauty for your family, use a ready-to-finish oval drop-leaf table with a removable top. Paint the top with wood sealer before stenciling. Fill in the design using a separate brush for each color, or wash the brush after each color application. Allow the paint to dry overnight.

Finish the tabletop with clear varnish, and polish it with paste wax.

Home Sweet Home Place Mats

Shown on pages 50 and 51. Finished size of each mat is 22x14 inches.

MATERIALS
For four place mats
1½ yards of prequilted muslin fabric

6¾ yards of 1-inch-wide French-fold bias tape in muslin color

2 packages of tan fabric dye

Muslin-colored thread

Water-erasable marking pen

Stencil cutting paper

Marking pen to draw registration marks

Stencil cutting knife

Stencil brushes

Masking tape

Acrylic paints as follows: Navy blue (lettering, rectangles on floral border, dots surrounding hearts, and roofs of houses); light blue (tulips); rust (house, geese feet and bills); black (chimneys and windows); white (chimney smoke, window trim, dots of floral border, geese); pine green (trees, leaves, stems); light green (all border dividers); brown (tree trunks, deer, floral border, tulip baskets, small heart leaves, stems); plum (small dots in flower centers); maroon (hearts)

INSTRUCTIONS
Soak the prequilted fabric in warm water to remove any fabric sizing. Dye the wet fabric according to the manufacturer's instructions on the dye package. Machine-dry and iron the fabric on the back side.

SEWING THE PLACE MATS: Enlarge the outline of the heart on page 58 onto paper. Transfer the shape to

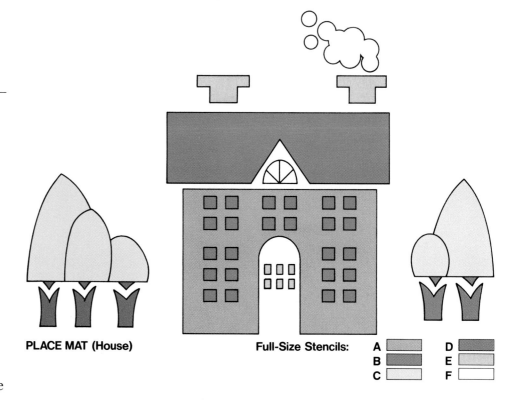

PLACE MAT (House)

Full-Size Stencils:

A · D · B · E · C · F

prequilted muslin fabric. Cut out four heart-shaped mats, adding ¼ inch all around.

Bind mats with the French-fold bias tape, starting at the lower left front side. With right sides facing, and using a ¼-inch seam allowance, sew around the entire heart shape. Miter the bias tape at the top and bottom points. Turn the bias to the back side and hand-stitch in place.

CUTTING THE STENCILS: The stencil patterns, *above* and *opposite*, are full size.

Cut one stencil for each color and design. Draw registration marks on each stencil to ensure placement accuracy when stenciling.

The X markings on the Home Sweet Home, the cross hatch markings on the tulip baskets, the fence design under the tulip baskets, and

the stems of the leaves between the lower row of hearts are added free-hand with a fine-tip artist's brush after the stenciling is completed. No stencil is cut for these areas.

Stencil the designs in rows, referring to the placement diagram on page 58. Allow each color to dry thoroughly before continuing to the next painted area.

To stencil the checkerboard motif, do the top row first; allow to dry thoroughly. Drop the stencil down one row, lining up the top with the bottom of the previous row. Shift the squares one to the right or left. Stencil the second row and allow the fabric to dry thoroughly.

TO HEAT-SET THE DESIGN: Place a paper towel on top of the mat. Using a hot iron, carefully press each mat. Hand washing is recommended.

PLACE MAT (Lettering)

**PLACE MAT
(Bottom Section)**

PLACE MAT (Top Section)

**Full-Size
Stencils:** A B C D E F

57

HOME-SWEET-HOME PLACE MAT DIAGRAM AND HEART PATTERN

1 Square = 1 Inch

Wooden Trees

Shown on pages 50 and 51. Finished sizes of trees (with base and heart top) are 12, 15, and 19 inches.

MATERIALS
30 inches of 2x12-inch select pine
10 inches of 4x4-inch pine
Saber saw
3 inches of ¼-inch-diameter wooden dowel
7 inches of ½-inch-diameter wooden dowel
3½ inches of ¾-inch-diameter wooden dowel
Drill with ¼-, ½-, and ¾-inch drill bits
Crafts glue
Red and green acrylic paint
Artist's brush
Sandpaper
Antiquing glaze
Matte-finish clear acrylic

INSTRUCTIONS
Enlarge the patterns, *opposite,* and transfer the tree and heart shapes to paper. (The pattern is given full size for the small tree and heart.) Cut out the patterns. Trace around the patterns on pine. Using a saber saw, cut out the trees and hearts.

Drill a ¼-inch hole ½ inch deep in the top of the tree and the bottom of the heart.

Sand all edges and paint the entire tree green and the heart red.

Sand again; brush on an antiquing glaze. Allow the glaze to stand for a few minutes; wipe away excess glaze with soft cloth.

Spray trees and hearts with matte-finish clear acrylic. Cut a 1-inch length of ¼-inch-diameter dowel. Glue one end in bottom of heart and top of the tree.

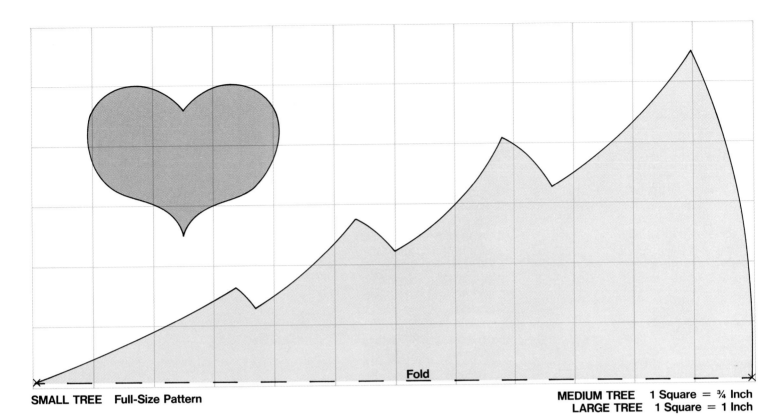

SMALL TREE   Full-Size Pattern

Fold

MEDIUM TREE   1 Square = ¾ Inch
LARGE TREE   1 Square = 1 Inch

TO MAKE THE BASE: Cut one block of wood as follows for each tree: 2½x2½ inches (small); 3x3 inches (medium); 3½x3½ inches (large). Cut a piece of ½-inch-diameter dowel 3½ inches long for the trunks of the small and medium trees. Cut a piece of ¾-inch-diameter dowel 3½ inches long for the trunk of the large tree.

Using a ½-inch drill bit for the small and medium trees, or a ¾-inch drill bit for the large tree, make a hole 1⅛ inches deep in the bottom of the tree and the top center of each base. Glue the dowel in the tree and the base to hold the two together. Leave a 1¼-inch section of the dowel showing between the tree and the base to represent the tree trunk.

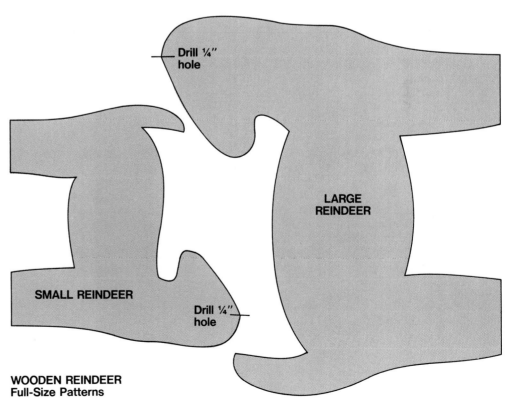

Drill ¼" hole

LARGE REINDEER

SMALL REINDEER

Drill ¼" hole

WOODEN REINDEER
Full-Size Patterns

59

Wooden Reindeer

Shown on pages 50 and 51.
Finished reindeer are 2½ and 3½ inches tall.

MATERIALS
Scraps of 1-inch pine
Drill with ⅛- and ¼-inch drill bits
Saber saw
¼-inch ribbon
Dried twigs (antlers)
Crafts glue
Red acrylic paint
Artist's brush
Sandpaper; tracing paper
Antiquing glaze
Matte-finish clear acrylic

INSTRUCTIONS
Transfer the full-size patterns on page 59 onto tracing paper. Cut out the patterns. Trace around patterns on pine. Using a saber saw, cut out reindeer.

Drill a ¼-inch-diameter hole in the top of the head of the large deer for the antlers. Drill a ⅛-inch-diameter hole in the head of the small deer. Holes should be about ⅛ inch deep.

Sand all edges and paint the entire reindeer red. Sand again; brush on an antiquing glaze. Allow glaze to stand for a few minutes; wipe off excess glaze with soft cloth.

Spray reindeer with matte-finish clear acrylic. Find a twig from a tree or bush that measures approximately 3 inches in length. Pick one that has a lot of branches coming together so that it resembles antlers. Glue "antlers" in place. Tie ribbon around reindeer's neck.

Barnyard Wreath

Shown on page 52.
Finished size is 14-inch diameter.

MATERIALS
14-inch plastic foam wreath
Sphagnum moss
Scraps of ½-inch pine
½-inch- and ⅛-inch-diameter dowel (fence)
Acrylic paints in brown, cream, black, gold, medium blue, light blue, red, peach
Antiquing glaze
Clear acrylic varnish
Wood glue
Floral picks
Drill and ⅛-inch drill bit
Band saw

INSTRUCTIONS
Enlarge farm animal, barn, and farmer patterns, *opposite,* onto paper. Cut out shapes. Draw around all pattern pieces on pine.

Use a band saw to cut out all pieces. Sand surfaces smooth. Paint details with acrylic paints, referring to the color photograph on page 52 for guidance.

Allow acrylic paints to dry thoroughly. Coat each piece with antiquing glaze; wipe off excess glaze and allow pieces to dry. Spray each shape with clear acrylic varnish.

Drill a small hole on the back side of each animal into which you can insert a florist's pick. Do not drill too deeply. Glue a floral pick into the back of each shape. Stick the other end of the pick into the wreath at the appropriate location. Refer to the photograph on page 52.

Since the barn is so large and heavy, drill one hole on each side of the back and glue in short pieces of dowel to hold the barn in place on the wreath. Glue the farmer to the barn with his legs extending below the bottom edge of the barn.

For the fence
Cut four pieces of ½-inch dowel each 3 inches long. Cut two pieces of ⅛-inch dowel each 13 inches long. Drill two holes completely through each 3-inch dowel. Holes should be 1 inch in from each end of the dowel.

Rub antiquing glaze over the fence pieces to "age" the wood.

Slide the ⅛-inch dowel through the ½-inch dowel "posts." A drop of glue on the back side will hold the fence pieces together.

Drill a hole and insert a pick in the back side of each of the two end posts. Position the fence and fasten it securely on the wreath.

Geese and Cow Hooked Rug

Shown on page 53.
Finished size is 24x36 inches.

MATERIALS
Wool fabric as follows: Light and dark oatmeal, black, gray check, brown, soft peach, gold, rust, rose tweed, white, green tweed
30x40 inches of burlap
Rug hooking tool
Rug frame (optional)

INSTRUCTIONS
Enlarge the pattern on page 62 onto paper. Transfer the design to burlap. Mount burlap in rug frame.

Select wool fabrics in a variety of textures, from smooth flannel to checks, stripes, and tweeds. Cut all wool into ¼-inch strips.

(*Note:* A printed burlap with pre-cut wool can be purchased from the designer, Joan Moshimer, Box 351, Kennebunkport, ME 04046.)

For the cow
Start by hooking the cow's head using oatmeal wool. The eye, nostril,
continued

BARNYARD WREATH

BARN

HORSE

GOOSE

SHEEP

COW

FARMER

PIG

Drill hole for tail

CHICKEN

1 Square = 1 Inch

61

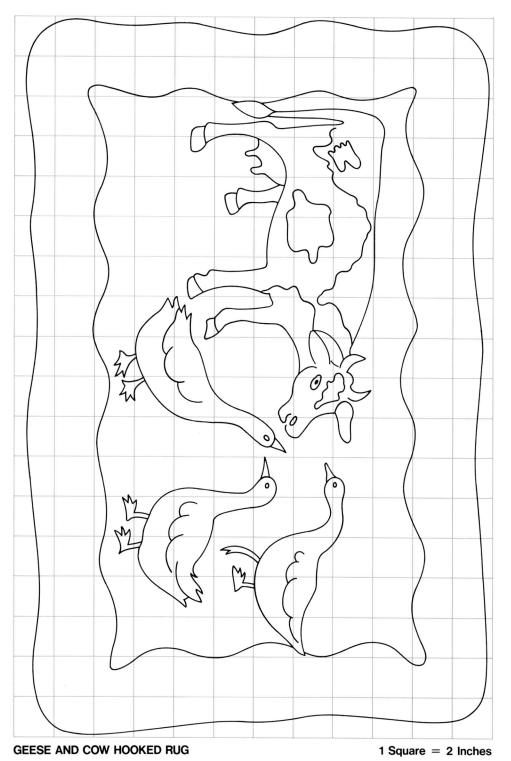

GEESE AND COW HOOKED RUG　　　　1 Square = 2 Inches

and mouth are worked in black. The patch on the forehead is black, surrounded by a line of black and white tweed. Hook the horns in brown.

Finish all the black spots on the body, surrounding each with a few rows of black and white tweed. Refer to the color photograph on page 53 for placement.

Fill in remainder of the body with oatmeal wool. Work the udder with peach wool and hooves with black.

For the geese
Hook the bodies of the geese in white and oatmeal. Outline the wings with dark oatmeal. Make the beaks gold, and feet and legs rust. Add one black dot for each eye.

For the background
Hook a single line of white tweed border as marked on the pattern. Next to this line, hook a single line of tan. Fill in the background with a rose-colored tweed.

For the border
Blend colors in the rows of the border as desired. The photograph on page 53 will provide guidance if you want the rug to look exactly like the one pictured. Or, this is a good opportunity to be creative and make the rug coordinate with other accessories in your home.

Remove the rug from the frame.

To bind the rug
Cut wool fabric on the bias in 2-inch-wide strips. Run a row of machine stitching, using a matching thread, about ⅓ inch from one edge. This will make it easier to sew on by hand, since you can easily turn the binding edge under at the row of machine stitching. In sewing the other edge to the back of the rug, do not try to turn the raw edges of the bias under. Take small hemming stitches and the raw edge will be covered without any bulk.

Needlepoint Cat

Shown on page 53.
Finished size is 12 inches tall.

MATERIALS
14x16 inches of 11-count canvas
3-ply Paternayan Persian wool yarn
  in colors listed on the color key
Tapestry needle
Masking tape
Waterproof marking pen
¼ yard of black cotton piping
½ yard of black velveteen or
  suitable substitute (backing)
Black sewing thread
Polyester fiberfill

INSTRUCTIONS
Transfer the needlepoint chart on page 64 to graph paper or work directly from our pattern.

Press the canvas flat with a dry iron. Bind all of the edges with masking tape to keep the canvas from raveling and to prevent yarns from catching in the rough edge of the canvas as you stitch. If desired, mount the canvas in a frame for stitching to minimize distortion as you work.

Use two strands of yarn throughout. Work all small details in continental stitches. Work the larger areas in basket-weave stitches. (See the stitch diagram on page 186.)

When the entire cat is stitched, work two rows of black continental stitches around the outer edges so that none of the cat design is lost when the pillow is sewn together.

Block the finished needlepoint before assembling the pillow.

TO ASSEMBLE THE PILLOW: Lay the needlepoint on the velveteen backing with right sides facing. Baste the pieces together to prevent shifting. Machine-stitch around the outlines of the cat, running the machine stitches just inside the two additional black rows of needlepoint stitches. Leave the bottom open for turning. Stitch again. Trim excess canvas and velveteen close to the stitching. Carefully turn the cat right side out and press lightly. Stuff the cat with polyester fiberfill and slip-stitch the bottom edges closed.

Oval Drop-Leaf Game Table

Shown on pages 54 and 55.
Finished size of tabletop as shown is 30x40 inches.

MATERIALS
Oval drop-leaf table with unpainted
  top
Crafts knife
Pencil
Stencil cutting paper
Chalk pencil
Masking tape
Fine sandpaper
Paste wax
Soft cloth
Clear sealer
Clear satin-finish varnish
Stencil brushes
Stencil paints in the following
  colors: Hunter green, dark
  brown, maroon, ecru, camel,
  slate blue

INSTRUCTIONS
Note: The table used in the project on pages 54 and 55 is made by Habersham Plantation. For a store near you, write to Habersham Plantation Corp., Box 1209, Taccoa, GA 30577.

PREPARING THE TABLE: Remove the top from the base. Separate the leaves and the center of the top.

Paint the base blue. (Table shown came with blue base and natural top.) Base-coat the three sections of the tabletop with two coats of sealer, sanding lightly between coats. Mark the lengthwise and crosswise centers of the outstretched tabletop with a chalk pencil.

CUTTING STENCILS: The stencil patterns on pages 65–67 are full size. Cut one stencil for each color to be used. The solid lines on the patterns are cutting lines. Place the cutting material over the design, and mark the cutting lines with a sharp pencil. Cut and label each stencil.

STENCILING THE DESIGNS: *Note:* Only dry brushes should be used. Overnight drying is necessary between washing the brush and starting with a new color.

Stencil the center checkerboard motif first.

To make the checkerboard stencil, draw four 1⅛x1⅛-inch squares, placed in a row and spaced 1⅛ inches apart, onto stencil material. Cut squares.

Draw a chalk line 1⅛ inches below the horizontal center line. Place the bottom edge of the checkerboard stencil along the chalk line. Tape the stencil in place and stencil with maroon stencil paint. Remove and reverse the stencil so that the painted and unpainted squares are offset. Place the bottom edge of the row along the top edge of the squares just stenciled and repeat. Repeat this pattern until there are eight rows of checkerboard squares. The checkerboard area should measure 9x9 inches when completed. When all of the maroon paint is dry, go back and stencil the blue squares.

Stencil the remainder of the center area. Allow each color to dry before painting the next.

Draw the large heart around entire center motif; lightly stencil only the outer edge with slate blue paint.

Stencil the drop-leaf sides and the heart-and-leaf scalloped border.

continued

NEEDLEPOINT CAT

1 Square = 1 Stitch

COLOR KEY

⊠	**Black**	**221**	ⓘ	**Brown**	**730**	☐	**White**	**262**
◎	**Rust**	**833**	⊡	**Gold**	**753**	●	**Green**	**693**

OVAL DROP-LEAF GAME TABLE

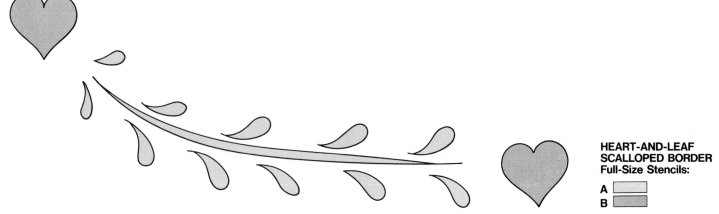

**HEART-AND-LEAF
SCALLOPED BORDER
Full-Size Stencils:**

A
B

Fold

Match Line AB

B

A

**DROP-LEAF MOTIF
Full-Size Stencils:**

A
B
C
D

FINISHING THE TABLE: Paint all edges of the table with ecru paint and a fairly dry brush. Use very light brush pressure and "dust" the color on the edges. Allow the paint to dry.

Using the stencil brush, dab over the ecru edging with slate blue, "frosting" the edges.

Allow the blue paint to dry 24 hours. Apply two coats of varnish. Dry and sand lightly between coats.

Apply two coats of paste wax and polish the finish with a soft cloth.

Reassemble the table.

Match Line AB

B

A

TABLE CENTER
Full-Size Stencils:

A
B
C
D

COUNTRY CRITTERS THAT KIDS WILL LOVE

How delightful the imagination when crafters are working on a holiday gift for a favorite child (or adult)!

Y ou can quickly change simple supplies like fabric scraps, instant tea, and paint into wondrous country treasures.

The pillows, *above*, are stenciled and tea-dyed. A homespun ruffle adds the finishing touch.

The friends in the haymow, *right*, have taken an afternoon off from mouse-chasing to relax with their friend, Ruth Rabbit.

Instructions for projects in this chapter begin on page 72.

COUNTRY CRITTERS
THAT KIDS WILL LOVE

Who ever said cats and dogs are incompatible? In the pillow design, *left,* the kitten cuddles the puppy with affection. Stencil the body design first. Then embroider body outlines and facial features. Fasten a fabric bow securely at each neckline. Ruffle the pillow to match.

Cat and dog stuffed toys, *below,* are patterned after the pillow. Faces are embroidered before the toys are assembled. And the children, *opposite,* each wear their favorite animal appliquéd on their pajamas.

Rabbit and Cats Stuffed Toys

Shown on pages 68 and 69.
Finished size is 23 inches tall *each*.

MATERIALS

For one rabbit or cat body

¼ yard of muslin fabric
Instant tea
Ecru sewing thread
Polyester fiberfill
Acrylic paints in gray and light
　brown
Permanent marking pens in black
　and dark brown

For the clothes

½ yard each of muslin and print
　fabric
Thread
Scraps of lace and ribbon
¼-inch elastic

INSTRUCTIONS

TO TRANSFER THE PATTERN: Enlarge the pattern, *opposite,* to full size. The parallel wavy lines indicate areas you must lengthen to the specifications given on the pattern pieces. The measurements given are the total overall lengths after you've added the extensions.

　Cut out all pattern pieces, adding ¼-inch seam allowances to all sides.

TEA-DYEING THE MUSLIN: All the fabrics used in these projects have been "aged" with tea stains.

　Mix 6 tablespoons of instant tea to each ⅓ cup of cold water. Dip the muslin and cotton print fabrics into the tea. Wring out the excess tea. Rinse the fabric in cold water. Vigorously wring out the water from the fabric. Dry the fabrics thoroughly. (Do not iron out the wrinkles you have created from squeezing the fabric. They add to the aged look of the dried fabric.)

CUTTING OUT THE PIECES: Transfer the patterns (legs, ears, arms, and head and body) to muslin fabric. Cut out all of the pieces.

SEWING THE BODY: The bodies of the cats and the rabbit are identical. The only change is in the ears. Note on the pattern that the ears are included with the cat's head pattern. To make the rabbit, note the cutting line marked on the top of the head pattern piece. The rabbit ears pattern is given separately, *opposite.*

For the rabbit

Note: In all instructions that follow, sew pieces with right sides facing using ¼-inch seams. Stitch around the entire head and body piece, leaving areas open for inserting the ears, arms, and legs. Turn the body right side out.

　Sew two ear pieces together; turn right side out. Repeat for second ear. Stitch in place to rabbit body.

　Sew arm pieces together; turn right side out. Stuff the paw and forearm section firmly. Machine-stitch across middle of right side of arm to form elbow. Stuff remaining arm pieces. Insert into body and top-stitch opening closed to secure arm in place.

　Firmly stuff entire head and body.

　Sew leg sets together following instructions for arms. Insert in bottom of body and seam across lower part of body, closing entire body opening.

For the cat

Follow the instructions, *above,* for assembling the rabbit. Omit the long-ear construction since the cat's ears are part of the body pattern.

Painting the rabbit or cat

The bodies of the rabbit and cats on pages 68 and 69 have been painted with a sponge to give the surface a textured appearance. Refer to the photograph for color guidance.

　When the body paint is thoroughly dry, add the facial features. Use a permanent marking pen or a fine-tipped brush and acrylic paint.

For the clothes

DRESS: Cut out the dress bodice pieces. (*Note:* There are two cutting lines: one for the drop-waist dress, one for the regular-waist dress. The sleeve pattern given is for short sleeves. Extend the sleeve 3 inches for a long-sleeved dress.)

　With right sides facing, stitch along the top of the arm up to the neck area, stopping at the X marked on the pattern piece. Turn under the hemline of the sleeve. Sew a piece of elastic inward ¾ inch from the edge of the sleeve. Pull the elastic to gather the sleeve as you stitch. With right sides facing, stitch up the side, and down the underside of the sleeve.

　Cut a rectangle of fabric 18 inches long by 8 inches wide (drop waist) or 18x10 inches (regular waist). With right sides facing, stitch the back seam of the skirt together. Machine-sew a ¼-inch hem along the bottom of the skirt. Gather to fit the dress bodice. Turn the dress right side out. Embellish with lace and ribbons where desired. (The photograph on pages 68 and 69 will serve as a guide.)

COLLAR: Cut two collar pieces. With right sides facing, stitch around entire collar, leaving openings marked on the pattern for turning. Clip curves. Turn the collar right side out; stitch opening closed. Add a bow, or appliqué an old-fashioned heart to the collar.

continued

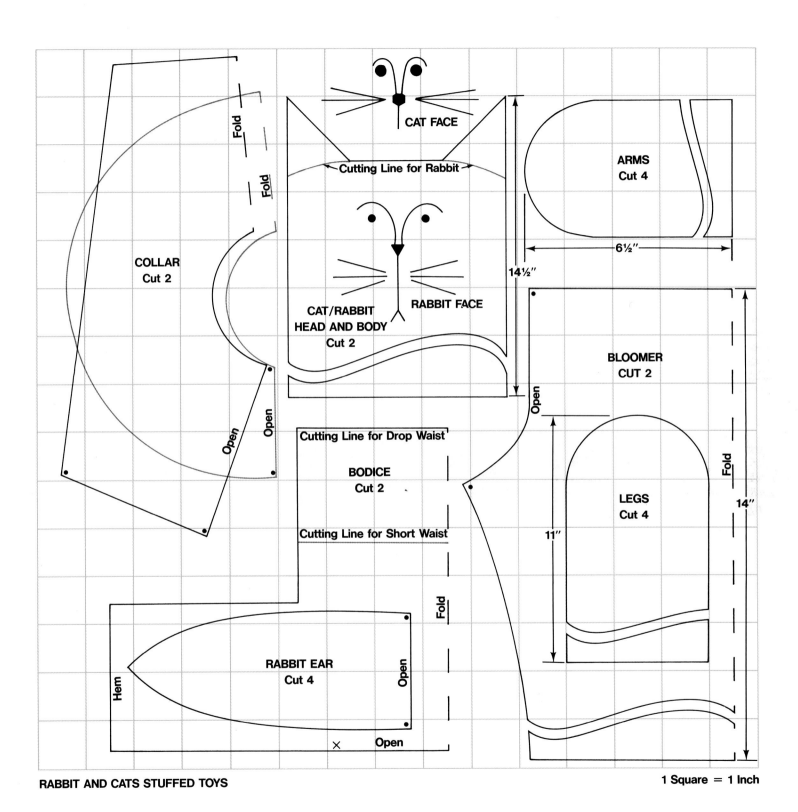

CAT FACE

←Cutting Line for Rabbit→

RABBIT FACE

CAT/RABBIT HEAD AND BODY Cut 2

COLLAR Cut 2

Fold

Fold

Open

Open

14½"

ARMS Cut 4

6½"

BLOOMER CUT 2

Open

Fold

14"

Cutting Line for Drop Waist

BODICE Cut 2

Cutting Line for Short Waist

Fold

LEGS Cut 4

11"

RABBIT EAR Cut 4

Hem

Open

× Open

RABBIT AND CATS STUFFED TOYS

1 Square = 1 Inch

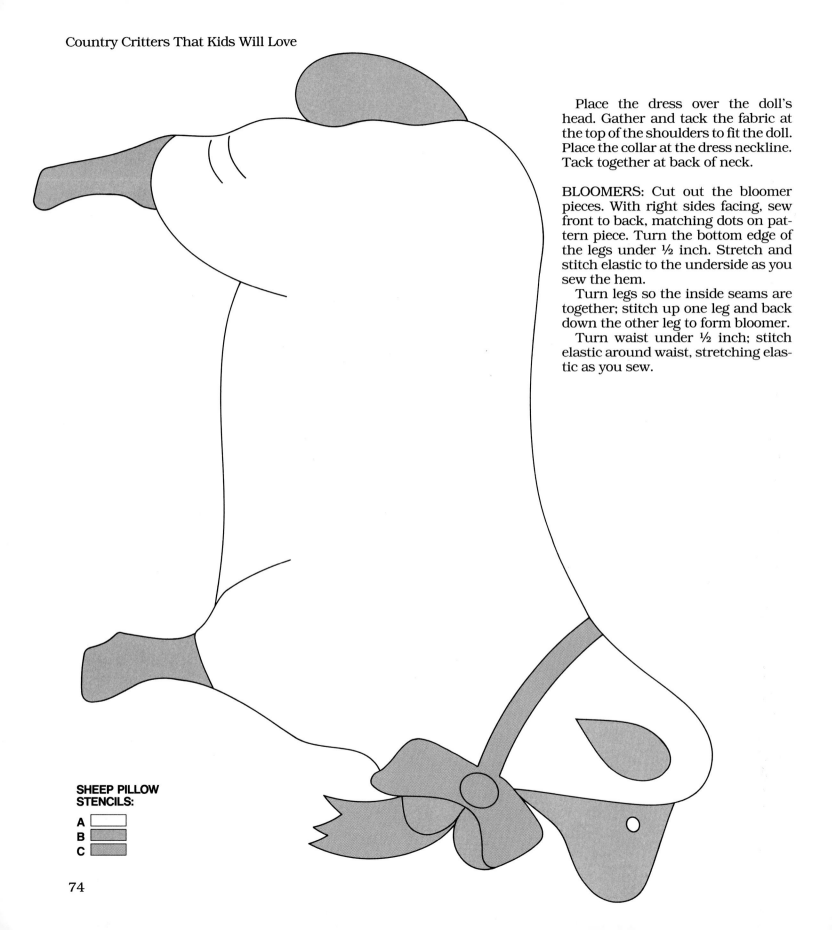

Place the dress over the doll's head. Gather and tack the fabric at the top of the shoulders to fit the doll. Place the collar at the dress neckline. Tack together at back of neck.

BLOOMERS: Cut out the bloomer pieces. With right sides facing, sew front to back, matching dots on pattern piece. Turn the bottom edge of the legs under ½ inch. Stretch and stitch elastic to the underside as you sew the hem.

Turn legs so the inside seams are together; stitch up one leg and back down the other leg to form bloomer.

Turn waist under ½ inch; stitch elastic around waist, stretching elastic as you sew.

SHEEP PILLOW STENCILS:

A ☐
B ☐
C ☐

Stenciled Cat
And Sheep Pillows

Shown on page 68.
Finished size of each pillow is
13½x15½ inches, excluding ruffle.

MATERIALS
For one pillow
18x20-inch piece of muslin fabric
1½ yards backing/ruffle fabric
Stencil paper
Stencil knife
Acrylic paints
Stencil brush
Polyester fiberfill
Instant tea

INSTRUCTIONS
CUTTING THE STENCIL: Patterns,
right and *opposite,* are full size.
Transfer patterns to tissue paper.
Tape to cutting board. Lay stencil paper over pattern; tape in place. Cut
one stencil for each color area.

For the cat stencil
Cut one stencil for heart, one for collar and eyes, and one for cat body.

For the sheep stencil
Cut one stencil for sheep body; one
for face, ears, tail, feet, and inside of
bow; and one for the main part of the
bow and collar.

You may cut your own stencils for
the numbers and the checkerboard
border. Or, you may choose to purchase commercial stencils that are
readily available for both.

DYEING THE FABRIC: To give the
new muslin fabric a timeworn appearance, stir up a batch of strong
hot tea. Dip the fabric into the tea.
Wad the fabric into a ball, squeezing
out the excess tea. Rinse the fabric in
cold water and allow it to dry thoroughly. Do not iron the fabric. The
wrinkles will add to the aged appearance of the finished project.

continued

**CAT PILLOW
STENCILS:**

A
B
C

Position the stencil design for the body of the sheep or cat in the center of the muslin fabric; anchor it with masking tape at the corners. Put a small amount of paint into a can lid or paint tray. (Use light gray for the cat body, dark blue for the collar, and rust for the heart. Use white for the sheep body; black for the nose, ears, feet, tail, and inside of bow; and rust for the bow and collar.) Dip the tip of the stencil brush into the paint and remove the excess by dabbing the brush onto a piece of paper. The secret to successful stenciling is to use a nearly dry brush; this produces the best print.

Hold the brush perpendicular to the stencil and use an up-and-down motion to apply the paint. Do not stroke or drag the paint across the stencil, or it will smear under the template edges. To achieve the best results, work from the edges of the stencil toward the center. When done, carefully remove the stencil.

Allow each color of paint to dry before going to the next stenciling color. Wipe the stencil each time you move it to prevent paint smears.

For the cat
With an artist's brush and dark gray, hand-paint the remainder of the facial features and the detail in the ears and on the body.

For the sheep
Dip the brush into black paint. Dab it on scrap paper until almost all of the paint is out of the brush. Gently add black shading around the edge of the sheep body.

Finish the pillow by following the general instructions on page 187.

Cat and Dog Pillow

Shown on page 71.
Finished size is 13x13 inches, excluding the ruffle.

MATERIALS
16x16-inch piece of muslin fabric
1 yard of plaid fabric (ruffle and backing)
¼ yard small dot or print fabric (cording)
1¾ yards medium-weight cording
Embroidery floss in black, brown, and red
Embroidery needle
Acrylic paints in light brown, light gray, and winter white
Textile medium (to thin acrylics)
Small artist's brush
Polyester fiberfill

INSTRUCTIONS
The pattern, *opposite,* is full size. Trace the pattern onto tissue paper. Center and transfer the design onto the muslin fabric.

Paint the entire cat shape light gray; paint the dog shape light brown. (Thin the acrylic to one part textile medium to two parts acrylic paint. If you need a lighter shade of gray or brown, add a small part of winter white until you achieve the desired shade.)

Practice on fabric scraps. The color will run outside of the lines if you have too much paint in the brush. Tap the brush on scrap paper to get rid of the excess paint.

Allow the first color of paint to dry thoroughly before continuing to the second shade. With an iron on a very hot setting, press the painted fabric on the wrong side of the design to permanently set the paint. Move the iron around quickly to prevent scorching.

Embroider the body and face lines of the cat with three strands of black embroidery floss using outline stitches. Fill in the pupils of the eyes and the nose with black satin stitches. Use red floss and satin stitches to fill in the tongue area.

Embroider the body and face lines of the dog with three strands of brown floss using outline stitches. Fill in the pupils of the eyes and the nose with brown satin stitches. Use red floss and satin stitches to fill in the tongue area.

Use outline stitches and three strands of black floss to create the parallel lines along the lower portion of the pillow top. (Refer to the photograph on page 71 for placement.)

Press the pillow top on the wrong side. Attach a plaid fabric bow to the neck of each animal. (Refer to the photograph on page 71.)

Finish the pillow following the general instructions for pillows and sachets on page 187.

CAT AND DOG PILLOW
AND PAJAMA PATTERN
Full-Size Pattern

Cat and Dog Pajamas

Shown on page 70.

MATERIALS
Commercial nightgown or pajama
　pattern
Soft flannel fabric (yardage as
　specified in pattern)
Contrasting fabric for trimming
　(yardage as specified in pattern)
Buttons
Contrasting threads for appliqué
Embroidery floss in black, brown,
　and red
Fusible webbing

INSTRUCTIONS
Assemble the nightgown or pajamas
following pattern directions. Embellish with contrasting trim.

Trace either the cat or the dog
from the full-size pattern on page 77
onto tracing paper. Cut out the
shape. From fabric, cut out desired
shape.

Cut matching shape for each piece
from fusible webbing.

Position and fuse the cat or dog to
the nightgown or pajamas.

Machine-zigzag-stitch around the
shapes with matching threads.

Embroider the face lines of the cat
with three strands of black embroidery floss using outline stitches. Fill
in the pupils of the eyes and the nose
with black satin stitches. Use red
floss and satin stitches to fill in the
tongue area.

Embroider the face lines of the dog
with three strands of brown floss using outline stitches. Fill in the pupils
of the eyes and the nose with brown
satin stitches. Use red floss and satin
stitches to fill in the tongue area.

Add fabric or ribbon bows.

Cat and Dog Stuffed Toys

Shown on page 71.
Finished size of each toy is 10½
inches tall.

MATERIALS
½ yard *each* gray (cat) and brown
　(dog) broadcloth
⅓ yard red/green plaid fabric (bow)
Embroidery floss in black, dark
　brown, and pink
Size No. 3 perle cotton in gray and
　medium brown
Polyester fiberfill
Long soft-sculpture needle

INSTRUCTIONS
For the cat and dog
Patterns on pages 78–81 are full
size. Transfer them to tissue paper.

Use gray fabric for cat and brown
fabric for dog. Cut two front and two
back leg pieces on fold of fabric.
Open pieces; stitch together with
right sides facing. Leave an opening
for turning.

On doubled thickness of fabric
(right sides facing), lay out pattern
pieces for body and cat tail. Trace
around pieces, but do not cut
shapes.

Machine-stitch on drawn lines,
leaving areas marked "open" unstitched. Cut out each shape ¼ inch
outside drawn line. Clip all curves.

For the cat
Turn cat's tail right side out. Stuff
lightly. Machine-stitch detail lines.
Slip tail inside body through neck
opening, lining up straight edge of
tail to tail opening on body. Stitch
opening closed, encasing tail.

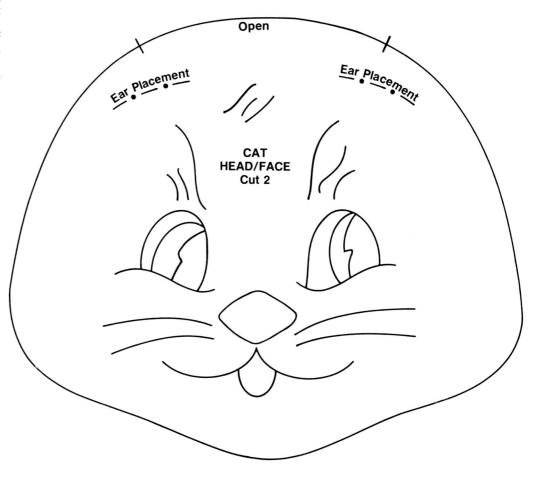

For cat and dog

Turn body right side out. Turn under top edge of neck ½ inch and baste. Stuff body firmly.

Stitch across toe of each of the four feet by matching two dots on seam line together, forming a triangle. Measure ½ inch down from tip of the triangle and stitch straight across. Turn legs right side out and stuff lower portion of leg firmly. Stuff upper portion less firmly. Blindstitch opening closed. (For cat only, use black floss and a long stitch to stitch three toe lines on each foot. Refer to photograph on page 71.)

Position and pin legs to body, matching X markings on pattern.

Stitch legs to body beginning at dot on back edge of leg, continuing across "bridge," and stopping at dot on other side of second leg. (Position back legs so back bottom of body sits on "bridge," folding legs forward.) Secure front portion of front and back legs to body by threading perle cotton through sculpture needle and stitching through body at X on one leg to X on leg on other side. Hide knots on inside portion of legs.

For the cat's face

Trace around face pattern on single thickness of fabric. Machine-stay-stitch along drawn lines. Transfer facial features and embroider lines with black floss, using satin stitches for nose and center of eyes, and outline stitches for remaining lines. Use pink floss to satin-stitch tongue. Place stitched fabric, embroidered side down, on another piece of gray fabric. Using previous stay stitching, sew two pieces of fabric together, leaving an opening as marked on the pattern. Trim fabric ¼ inch outside
continued

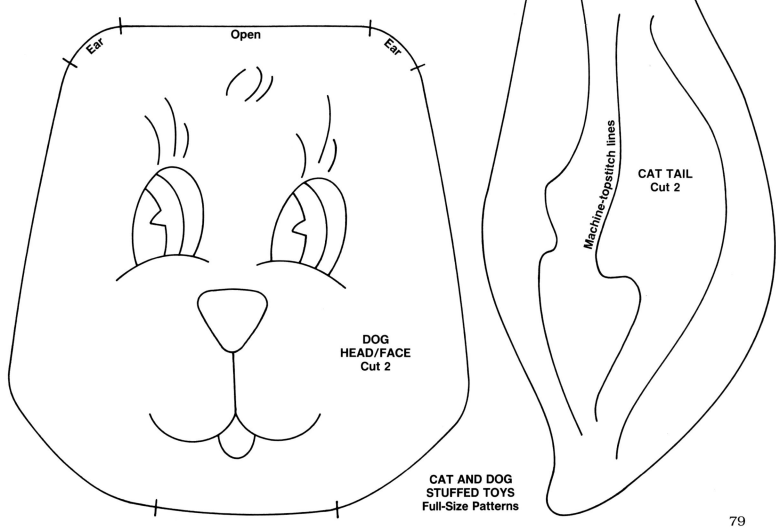

CAT AND DOG
STUFFED TOYS
Full-Size Patterns

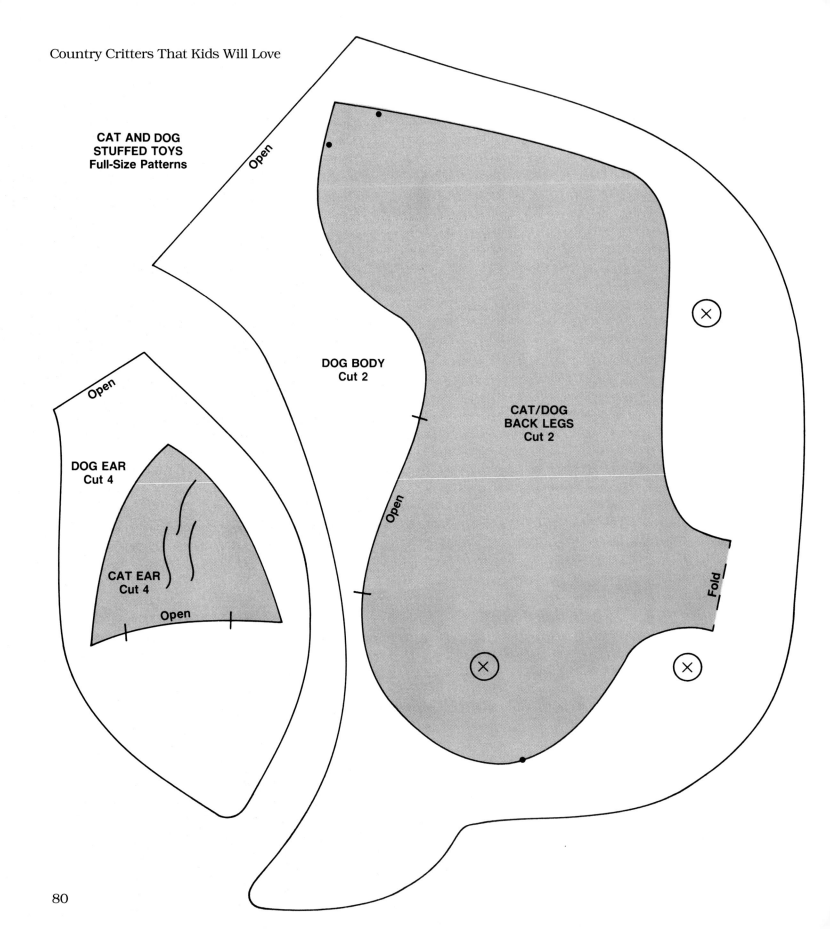

Country Critters That Kids Will Love

CAT AND DOG
STUFFED TOYS
Full-Size Patterns

Open

DOG BODY
Cut 2

Open

DOG EAR
Cut 4

CAT EAR
Cut 4

Open

CAT/DOG
BACK LEGS
Cut 2

Open

Fold

80

stitching; turn head right side out and stuff with fiberfill. Blindstitch opening closed. Turn ears right side out and stuff lightly. Embroider detail lines with black floss. Blindstitch opening closed. Position and blindstitch ears to head.

For the dog's face
Follow embroidery instructions for cat's face.

Turn the dog's ears right side out and stuff lightly. Sew across open ends. Position open edges of ears ¼ inch inside top corners of head as indicated on pattern. Baste ears in place. Place face, with ears in place, right side down on another piece of brown fabric. Proceed as for cat. After stuffing the head, fold ears toward front and tack into position along upper side of head.

For cat and dog
Center and pin head to neck and blindstitch neck edge to back of head. Remove basting stitches.

Flip the cat's tail up and attach it to the body.

For the bow
Cut a strip of plaid fabric 6x41 inches. Fold in half lengthwise, right sides facing. Sew diagonally across each end. Using a ¼-inch seam allowance, sew along raw edge, leaving an opening in center for turning. Trim away excess fabric on each end. Turn fabric right side out. Press lightly; blindstitch opening closed. Tie fabric ribbon around neck.

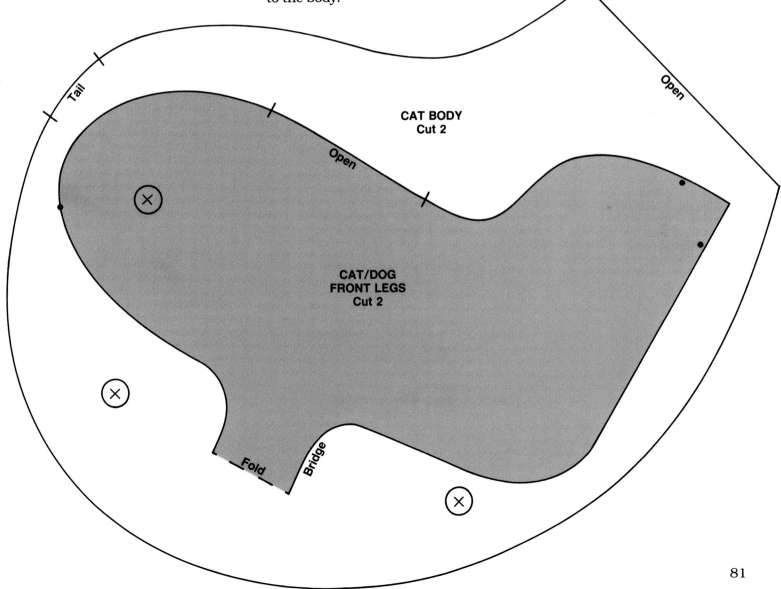

CAT BODY
Cut 2

CAT/DOG
FRONT LEGS
Cut 2

Tail

Open

Open

Fold

Bridge

CHRISTMAS PAPER CUTOUTS

Following the traditional techniques of early Pennsylvania Germans, snippets of paper folk art, or scherenschnitte, document events and proclaim sentiments for every occasion.

Derived from the German word *schnitte,* meaning "to cut," *scherenschnitte* is as popular today as it was with the immigrants who first introduced it to America.

You can create the beautiful Christmas keepsakes, *right,* with surgical scissors and paper. Transfer the patterns on pages 84 and 85 onto parchment or linen-finish tablet paper. Cut away the shaded areas and watch the

lambs and Nativity scene unfold. Hand-letter a special holiday message on the cuttings to personalize a gift.

In the design, *near right,* gentle lambs patiently await the birth of Christ. At *far right,* baby Jesus is greeted by the earth's creatures, while angels keep watch overhead.

Mounted on a dark background, and framed in a faux-finished frame, these images remind us of the true meaning of Christmas.

Christmas Crèche and Gentle Lambs Paper Cuttings

Shown on pages 82 and 83. Finished size of each cutting is 8x8 inches mounted as shown. (Frame size not included.)

MATERIALS
Linen-finish tablet paper or
  parchment paper
Small, sharp surgical scissors
Tracing paper
No. 2 lead pencil
Teaspoon
White crafts glue
Contrasting background paper

INSTRUCTIONS
Note: Surgical scissors (especially those designed for eye surgery) are excellent for cutting. Such scissors have a straight cutting edge and pinpoint tips. If used on thin paper, they need not be sharpened often.

Always cut with the tips of the scissors, completely closing the tips at the end of every snip. This is a good habit to acquire, for you could tear your work by withdrawing opened scissors.

TRANSFERRING THE PATTERN: Trace the outline from the patterns, *below* and *opposite,* onto tracing paper. Use a soft (No. 2) lead pencil. Place the pencil-sketched side of the tracing paper next to the paper to be cut. Holding it firmly in place with your hand, and using the rim edge of

a teaspoon, stroke firmly along the pencil lines until the image clearly is transferred to the paper.

CUTTING THE DESIGN: Always cut away the inside areas of the design first. Cut the outside edge last. This allows you a larger area of paper to grasp while cutting the tiny inside openings.

FINISHING THE DESIGN: Turn the cutting over so that none of the pencil lines or finger marks show. Place a small dab of white glue on the underside and press the cutting in place on the background paper. (Any type of mat board or colored paper may be used, except construction paper, which will fade when exposed to light.)

Frame each design as desired.

Fold

CUT-PAPER LAMBS

Full-Size Pattern

CUT-PAPER CRECHE

Full-Size Pattern

A HOMESPUN HOLIDAY IN TENNESSEE

As night steals over the Blue Ridge Mountains, and big snowflakes drift quietly downward, this proud country home is aglow with the warmth of the holiday season.

Inside, the air is laced with the aromas of freshly baked breads and chocolate fudge pie. Each room is bursting at the seams with handmade decorations, homespun quilts, and cross-stitched samplers by the score.

On the big pine four-poster, *right,* a faded blue and rose Goose Chase Star Quilt brings back memories of Christmas at Grandma's. Make an heirloom quilt just like this one to pass down to loved ones in your family.

Turn the page for a closer look at the cross-stitch sampler, bandboxes, and tree ornaments.

Instructions and patterns for all projects begin on page 94.

Who said band-boxes have to be round or oval? The boxes, *below,* are proof that any shape will work. We chose two of our country favorites, the bunny and the duck, and made containers just the right size for those special small gifts—jewelry, potpourri, perfume—use your imagination.

A satin bow tied around the neck will keep the package sealed from curious hands.

There will be no doubt that your whole heart is in the sampler, *opposite.* Cross-stitched in dusty blues and soft browns, this wall hanging reminds us all there really is no place like home—especially during the holidays.

A HOMESPUN HOLIDAY
IN TENNESSEE

Spatter-painted tin farm animals and punched copper tulips filled with baby's-breath trim a tree and cozy up a bedroom corner, *left* and *opposite.*

Animal motifs are repeated in a pinafore, *opposite,* that will delight any young girl. Sew a dress and pinafore from a commercial pattern. Cut out a variety of animal shapes from assorted calico prints and appliqué them to the skirt.

Have fun making this easily pieced angel, *below,* to sit atop your tree. She holds her own little lamb tucked inside a miniature basket. Stitch a flock of the little sheep to use as decorations on packages or on the tree.

91

A HOMESPUN HOLIDAY
IN TENNESSEE

Sunflowers may be a bit out of season in December, but the magnificent quilt, *right,* looks very festive displayed across a pine harvest table.

There seems to be no rhyme or reason for the background color in this antique quilt, and that may well be part of its charm. Instructions give you yardage for random colors as shown, or for a more planned palette should you choose to make all blocks the same.

A variety of black and navy print fabrics, thrown against the mustard-yellow sunflower petals, makes a handsome contrast in a coverlet you can use in any room in your house.

The 77½x93-inch quilt shown here is perfect for a full-size bed. Adjust the number of blocks to make a twin- or queen-size quilt.

Goose Chase
Star Quilt

Shown on pages 86 and 87.
Finished quilt size is 71½x87¾
inches. Finished block size is 22¾
inches square.

MATERIALS
All yardages are for 44- to 45-
inch-wide fabric
Approximately 3¾ yards of
  assorted red, blue, black, and
  pink fabric scraps
3 yards of blue and white polka-dot
  fabric
Approximately 1½ yards of white
  print fabric scraps
¾ yard of red or pink fabric for
  binding
5½ yards of fabric for quilt back
90x108-inch quilt batting
Cardboard or plastic for templates
Graph paper

INSTRUCTIONS
Full-size patterns, *above right,* are
finished size; add ¼-inch seam allowances when cutting pieces from
fabric. Dimensions for other pieces
include seam allowances. Sew all
pieces with right sides facing, taking
¼-inch seams.

TO BEGIN: Trace and make cardboard or plastic templates for the
patterns, *above right.*

CUTTING INSTRUCTIONS: To cut
the patchwork pieces, draw around a
template with a pencil on the wrong
side of the fabric. Cut out the pieces,
adding ¼-inch seam allowances.
  From the assorted colored fabric
scraps, cut 684 D triangles and 288
A diamonds.
  From the white print fabric
scraps, cut 144 B triangles, 144 C
squares, and 412 E triangles.

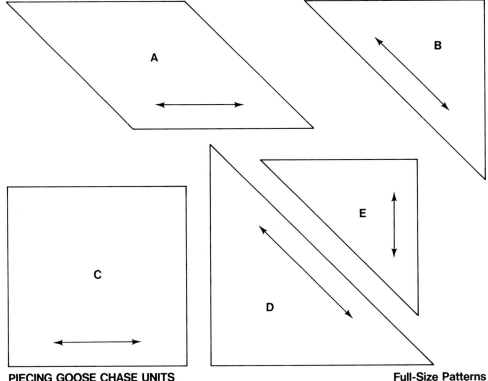

PIECING GOOSE CHASE UNITS　　　　　　　　**Full-Size Patterns**

From the blue and white polka-dot
fabric, cut 17 sashing strips, each
7x23¼ inches. Cut eight 7x7-inch
sashing squares. Cut six 10¼-inch
squares for the block centers. Measurements for these pieces include
seam allowances.

TO MAKE STARS: Choose two sets
of four matching diamonds for each
star. Alternating diamond fabrics,
join eight A diamonds into a star. Set
a B triangle into alternate openings
around the outside of the star. Set a
C square into the four corners to
complete the star.
  Piece 36 stars. Groups of four
matching stars are used for each
block; the remaining 12 stars are
setting squares.

TO MAKE THE GOOSE CHASE
UNITS: Referring to the piecing diagram, *opposite,* join three D triangles. Add an E triangle to each end.
  Make 228 Goose Chase units. Sets
of 24 matching units are used for
each block; the remaining units are
for the pieced sashing strips.

TO PIECE ONE BLOCK: Choose a set
of 24 matching Goose Chase units
and four matching stars for each
block.
  Referring to the block drawing, *opposite,* sew the Goose Chase units
into four strips of six units. Sew a
strip to opposite sides of a center
square. Sew a star onto the ends of
the remaining two strips; sew strips
to opposite sides of center square.
  Make six Goose Chase Star blocks.

TO SET THE QUILT TOP: Make
three pieced sashing strips by join-

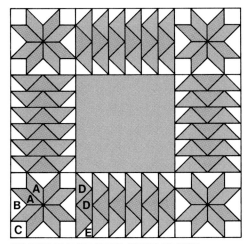

GOOSE CHASE STAR QUILT BLOCK

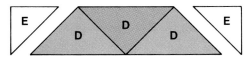

PIECING DIAGRAM FOR GOOSE
CHASE UNITS

ing groups of 14 Goose Chase units between 7x7-inch blue polka-dot squares.

Sew the quilt together in vertical rows, referring to the Quilt Piecing Diagram, *right*. To make the first row, join the three pieced sashing strips and three blue setting squares, beginning with a setting square and placing a square between strips.

In a similar manner, join three blue and white polka-dot sashing strips and four stars to make the second, fourth, and sixth rows.

To make the third and fifth rows, join three blocks and four blue and white polka-dot sashing strips, beginning and ending with a sashing strip and placing a strip between the blocks.

Join the rows.

FINISHING INSTRUCTIONS: To piece the quilt back, cut or tear the backing fabric into two long panels.

GOOSE CHASE STAR QUILT PIECING DIAGRAM

Split one panel in half lengthwise. Taking ½-inch seam allowances and matching selvage edges, sew a half panel to each side of the full panel. Trim off selvages so seam allowances are approximately ¼ inch. Press seams to one side.

Layer the quilt top, batting, and backing; baste. Quilt as desired.

Cut approximately 9 yards of 2½-inch-wide binding from the red binding fabric. Press the binding in half so it is 1¼ inches wide. Matching raw edges, stitch the binding to the quilt top. Trim excess batting and backing even with the quilt top. Stitch the folded edge of the binding to quilt back.

Hearts Sampler

Shown on page 89.
Finished size of design is 10x13 inches. Framed, as shown, finished size is 18x21 inches.

MATERIALS

14x17 inches of 18-count Aida cloth or any even-weave fabric with approximately 18 threads per inch
Embroidery floss in the colors listed on the color key, *opposite*

INSTRUCTIONS

PREPARING THE PATTERN: Chart the complete pattern, *right*, onto graph paper using felt-tip markers. Or, work directly from our pattern. (The shaded stitches on the portion of the pattern on page 97 indicate where the pattern on page 96 overlaps. *Do not repeat these stitches.*)

TO STITCH THE DESIGN: Separate the embroidery floss and use three strands of floss for working the cross-stitches.

Begin working 2 inches down from the top and 2 inches in from the left. This will leave 2 inches of plain fabric on all sides for mounting the finished needlework.

Stitch each counted cross-stitch over one thread of Aida fabric.

TO FINISH THE SAMPLER: If necessary, lightly press the stitchery on the back side of the fabric. Frame as desired.

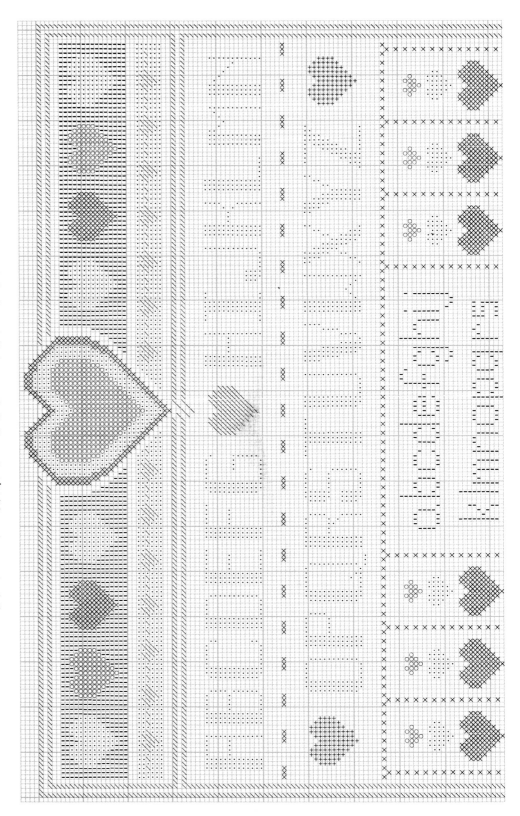

COLOR KEY

	DMC	Bates
◯ Light Brown	950	0376
· Medium Brown	3064	0379
⊠ Dark Brown	632	936

	DMC	Bates
⊞ Light Blue	932	976
⊡ Medium Blue	931	977
⊿ Dark Blue	930	978

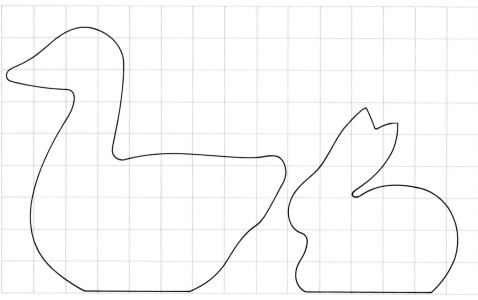

ANIMAL BANDBOXES   1 Square = 1 Inch

Animal Bandboxes

Shown on pages 86–87, and 88.

MATERIALS
Artist's mat board or illustration
  board
Printed paper, wallpaper, or fabric
  for covering box
Paper or fabric for lining
Crafts glue
Utility knife with sharp blade
Metal straightedge
Emery board or medium sandpaper
Paintbrush (for spreading glue)
Artist's brush
2 spring-type clothespins

INSTRUCTIONS
TO MAKE THE BASE: Enlarge the duck and rabbit patterns, *above,* onto paper. (Follow these same instructions to make any shape of bandbox.) Trace the shape onto the right side of the mat board. Cut out the shape with a utility knife and smooth the edges with an emery board or sandpaper.

TO MAKE THE BOX SIDE BAND: Cut a strip of mat board that measures 2½ inches wide and ¾ inch to 1 inch longer than the circumference of the base. Cut out the strip using a utility knife and metal straightedge. Sand the edges.

Cut a strip of printed paper or fabric 2 inches wider and 2 inches longer than the side band. Using crafts glue lightly thinned with water, center the paper or fabric strip over the band and glue in place. Smooth out all wrinkles or air bubbles as you go. Turn the band over; paint the edges of the paper or fabric with the crafts glue and press in place on the back of the band. Let the paper- or fabric-covered band dry thoroughly.

ATTACHING BASE AND SIDES: Place the base wrong side up on the table. Gently bend the side band around the base. Be careful not to let the band crease. Overlap the ends and be sure the band fits snugly all

the way around the base. Mark the overlap with a pencil mark.

Remove the band; glue overlapping ends together, holding the overlap in place with a clothespin until the glue is completely dry.

Cut a piece of paper or fabric 1 inch larger than the base. Cover the bottom of the base with glue, then center the paper or fabric over the base and smooth it in place. Place a weight (a book will do) on top of the base to keep it flat; allow the base materials to dry thoroughly.

Snip the paper or fabric outside of the cardboard base at ½-inch intervals all around the base. Crease the tabs inward toward the base.

Place the band on the table, top edge up. Slip the bottom, covered side down, inside the band, pushing it down against the table. Place glue on the back of each tab, then press it to the side band of the box to firmly attach the side to the base. (You may need to ask someone to help you since the animal shape makes a lot more turns and curves than a normal round or oval bandbox.) Use an artist's brush to press the tabs smooth, adding more glue over the top to keep them in place. Allow the glue to dry thoroughly.

TO MAKE THE LID: Set the box base down on the right side of a piece of mat board. Trace around the box with a pencil. (*Note:* Leave a hairline gap between the edge of the box and the pencil mark.) Remove the box and even out the line, if necessary.

Cut out the top with a utility knife. Smooth all rough edges. Measure around the lid and cut out a 1¼-inch rim band following the directions for the side band.

Cover the top and rim band with paper or fabric, and assemble as for base and side band.

Line the box with paper or fabric, if desired.

Copper Tulip Ornaments

Shown on pages 86–87, and 91.
Finished size is 3¾x4¾ inches.

MATERIALS
Copper tooling foil
Clear nylon thread
⅛-inch-wide satin ribbon (½ yard
  for each tulip)
Baby's-breath
Hammer
Nail
Scrap of lumber
Ruler

INSTRUCTIONS
Transfer the full-size pattern, *right,*
onto paper. Cut out the paper tulip
shape. Lay the pattern on top of the
tooling foil; draw around the outside
shape of the tulip. Make two copper
tulips for each ornament. Do not cut
out the copper tulips at this point.

Lay the copper on top of the scrap
of lumber. Using a hammer and nail,
make a hole at each point marked
with a dot on the pattern. (*Note:* Only
the outside holes are made on the
back tulip piece. The heart and grid
marks are made only on the front
shape.)

Using a ruler and any blunt pointed instrument, draw the grid lines
on the background of the tulip
shape.

With clear nylon thread, lace the
front and back tulip together. Lace
only the area between A and B, leaving the top open.

Cut a piece of ribbon 18 inches
long. Run one end through the hole
indicated by a circled dot on the pattern. Knot the ribbon on the inside of
the tulip. Run the other end of the
ribbon through the hole marked on
the opposite side; knot the end to the
inside. Tie a bow at the top for hanging. Fill the tulip with baby's-breath
or dried flowers.

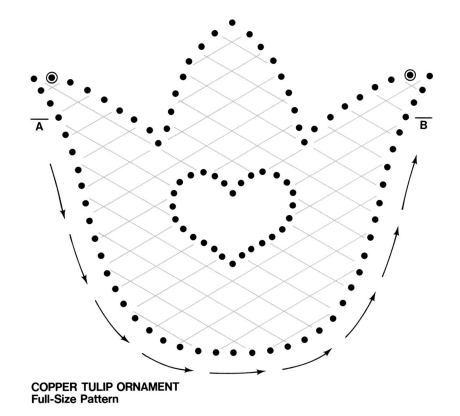

COPPER TULIP ORNAMENT
Full-Size Pattern

Appliquéd Dress

Shown on page 90.

MATERIALS
Commercial pattern for dress and
  pinafore (we used Butterick
  3442)
Fabric required for pattern of
  desired size
Scraps of assorted fabrics for
  appliqués
Thread
Zipper
Buttons
Hook-and-eye closure

Note: Notions may vary according
  to pattern.

INSTRUCTIONS
Select a commercial dress pattern
that has both a dress and pinafore
included. Stitch the dress and the
pinafore following the manufacturer's directions. Add cording and ruffles as desired.

From coordinating fabrics select
and cut out animal and heart appliqués. Full-size patterns are on pages
100 and 101. Reverse the patterns
so the animals are not all facing the
same direction.

Cut duplicate animal shapes from
fusible webbing. Arrange the fabric
shapes on the bodice and the skirt of
the pinafore. Place the webbing
shape between the animal cutout
and the pinafore fabric. Following
the manufacturer's suggestions,
iron over the animal cutouts to fuse
the two fabrics together. Machine-
satin-stitch around each of the animal shapes.

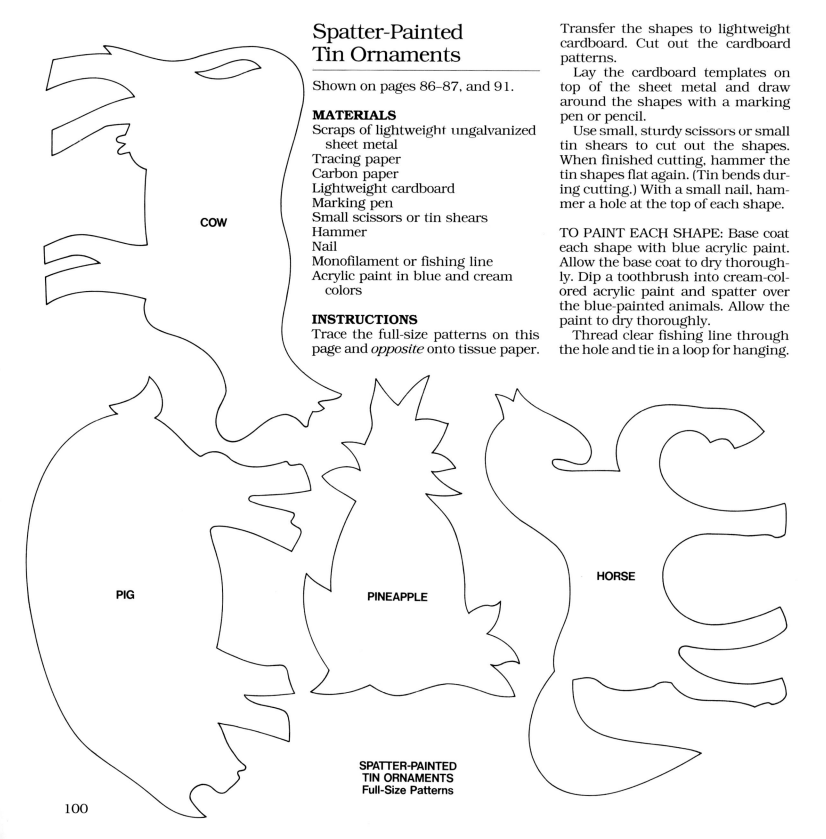

Spatter-Painted Tin Ornaments

Shown on pages 86–87, and 91.

MATERIALS
Scraps of lightweight ungalvanized
  sheet metal
Tracing paper
Carbon paper
Lightweight cardboard
Marking pen
Small scissors or tin shears
Hammer
Nail
Monofilament or fishing line
Acrylic paint in blue and cream
  colors

INSTRUCTIONS
Trace the full-size patterns on this
page and *opposite* onto tissue paper.

Transfer the shapes to lightweight
cardboard. Cut out the cardboard
patterns.
  Lay the cardboard templates on
top of the sheet metal and draw
around the shapes with a marking
pen or pencil.
  Use small, sturdy scissors or small
tin shears to cut out the shapes.
When finished cutting, hammer the
tin shapes flat again. (Tin bends during cutting.) With a small nail, hammer a hole at the top of each shape.

TO PAINT EACH SHAPE: Base coat
each shape with blue acrylic paint.
Allow the base coat to dry thoroughly. Dip a toothbrush into cream-colored acrylic paint and spatter over
the blue-painted animals. Allow the
paint to dry thoroughly.
  Thread clear fishing line through
the hole and tie in a loop for hanging.

COW

PIG

PINEAPPLE

HORSE

**SPATTER-PAINTED
TIN ORNAMENTS
Full-Size Patterns**

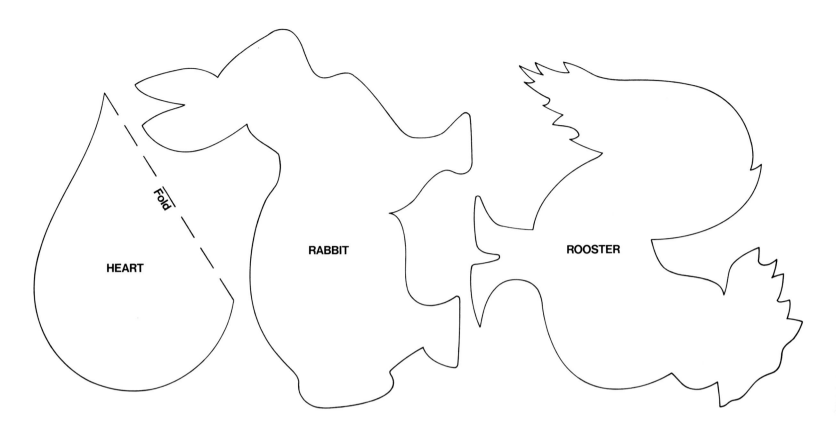

HEART

Fold

RABBIT

ROOSTER

Angel and Lamb Treetop Ornament

Shown on page 91.
Finished size of angel is 11 inches long.

MATERIALS
¼ yard of muslin
⅛ yard of cream-colored eyelet fabric
Scraps of calico, fleece, black knit (fuzzy), lace trim, narrow ribbon
Ecru wool roving (hair)
Quilting thread
Blue embroidery floss (sheep's eyes)
Fabric paint in brown, black, pink, dark blue, and medium blue
Artist's brush
Polyester fiberfill
Purchased 3-inch basket

INSTRUCTIONS
For the lamb
Transfer the full-size pattern on page 102 onto paper. Cut the lamb body from fleece. Cut face and ears from black knit.

Lay the right side of one face piece against the right side of one body piece. (See markings on pattern.) Join, using ¼-inch seams. Ease face piece to fit body piece.

Repeat for the other body and face pieces. Finger-press the seams open. Lay the seamed pieces together with right sides facing and sew around entire head/body shape with a ¼-inch seam allowance. Leave a 1½-inch opening at the bottom. Turn lamb right side out. Stuff firmly; stitch opening closed.

Place a dab of glue on the base of each ear. Fold the ear in half and hold it in place until the glue sets. Glue ear in place above lamb's face. Hold firmly until glue sets. Satin-stitch eyes with blue floss; tie a blue ribbon around the lamb's neck.

For the angel
Referring to the piecing diagram on page 102, piece and quilt the fabric for the front of the angel's body. Paint the hearts on the fabric.

Using the full-size patterns on pages 102 and 103, cut one angel body from the pieced fabric, and one from coordinating calico fabric for the back. Cut four sleeves. Piece the fabric for the sleeves or cut the sleeves from the calico. Do not quilt the sleeves.

From the muslin, cut the arms, head, and feet pieces. Cut the wings from cream-colored eyelet.

Transfer the facial features to the head shape; paint the features using fabric paints and an artist's brush. With right sides of the head pieces facing, using a ¼-inch seam allowance, stitch around the head. Leave a 1-inch opening at the bottom for turning. Turn right side out; stuff firmly. Stitch lengths of wool roving onto the angel's head, letting the stitch line become the hair part.

Shape the roving into braids, a bun, or twist. Use thread to secure the hair in place.

With right sides facing, stitch feet together in sets of two. Leave the end open for turning. Turn each foot right side out and stuff with fiberfill. Quilt toe lines on each foot. Place feet on the right side of the quilted angel body, overlapping the feet slightly. (Refer to the photograph on page 91 for placement.) Baste in place.

With right sides facing, stitch the wing pieces together. Leave the end open for turning. Turn right side out; stuff with fiberfill and stitch opening closed. Quilt along lines marked on the pattern pieces. Baste the wings in place along the top of the angel body.

Place the right sides of the body together and stitch, leaving an opening for turning. Turn; stuff firmly. Stitch opening closed.

Sew a sleeve to each arm piece. Cover wrist edge with lace. With the right sides together, sew arm pieces together in pairs, leaving an opening for turning. Turn right side out; stuff with fiberfill. Quilt finger lines.

Sew arms and head to angel body. Stitch basket to angel's hands and secure sheep in basket with glue.

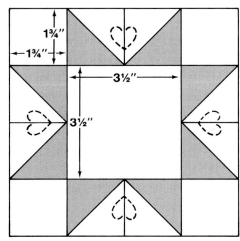

PIECING DIAGRAM FOR ANGEL BODY

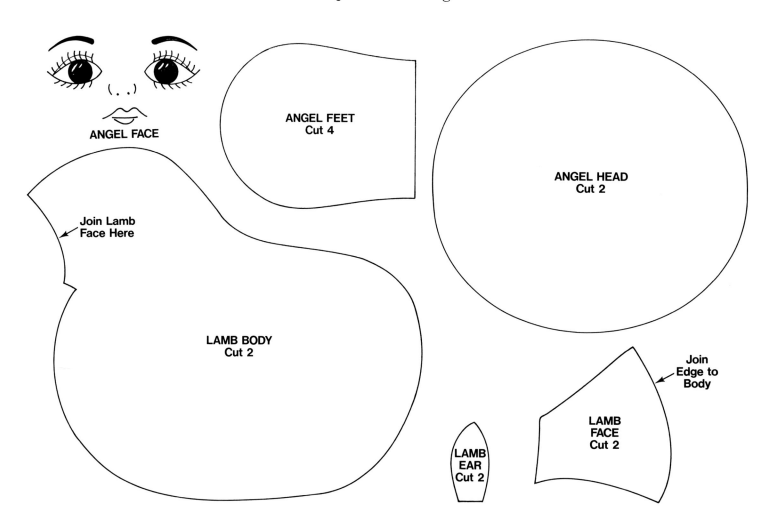

ANGEL FACE

ANGEL FEET
Cut 4

ANGEL HEAD
Cut 2

Join Lamb
Face Here

LAMB BODY
Cut 2

Join
Edge to
Body

LAMB
FACE
Cut 2

LAMB
EAR
Cut 2

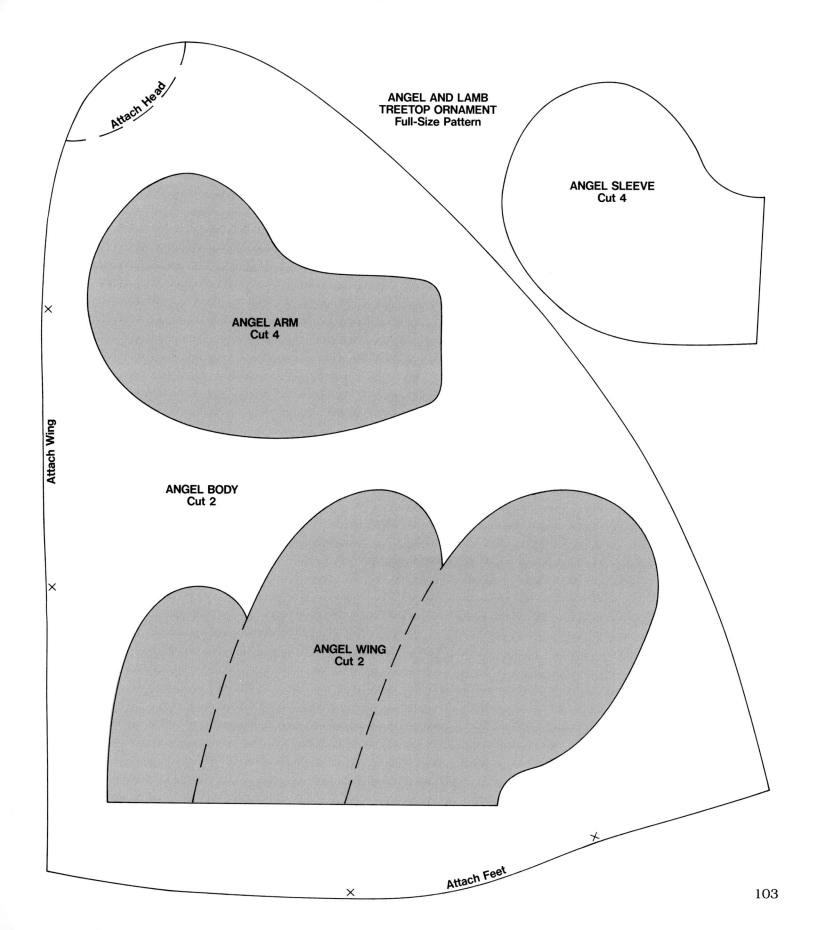

ANGEL AND LAMB
TREETOP ORNAMENT
Full-Size Pattern

ANGEL SLEEVE
Cut 4

Attach Head

Attach Wing

ANGEL ARM
Cut 4

ANGEL BODY
Cut 2

ANGEL WING
Cut 2

Attach Feet

103

Sunflower Quilt

Shown on pages 92 and 93.
Finished quilt size is 77½x93
inches. Each block is 15½ inches
square.

MATERIALS
**All yardages are for 44-inch-wide
fabric**
7½ yards of one fabric for making
all background blocks alike; or, 2
yards of red print fabric for 8
blocks, 3½ yards of navy print
fabric for 13 blocks, 1½ yards of
medium blue print fabric for 6
blocks, and 1 yard of gray print
fabric for 3 blocks
2¾ yards of green print fabric
1½ yards of yellow fabric
2¼ yards of assorted black and
white print and check fabrics
½ yard of black and white
pindotted fabric
1 yard of blue print fabric for
binding
6 yards fabric for quilt back
Quilt batting
Cardboard or plastic for templates

INSTRUCTIONS
Note: The antique quilt photo-
graphed on pages 92 and 93 is made
up of sunflowers with 13 points. The
instructions have been modified to
the usual number of 12 points for
simplicity in cutting and stitching.

Full-size patterns, *right,* are finished size; add ¼-inch seam allowances when cutting pieces from
fabric. Dimensions for other pieces
include seam allowances. Sew all
pieces with right sides facing, taking
¼-inch seams.

TO BEGIN: Trace and make cardboard or plastic templates for the
patterns, *right.* To cut the patchwork

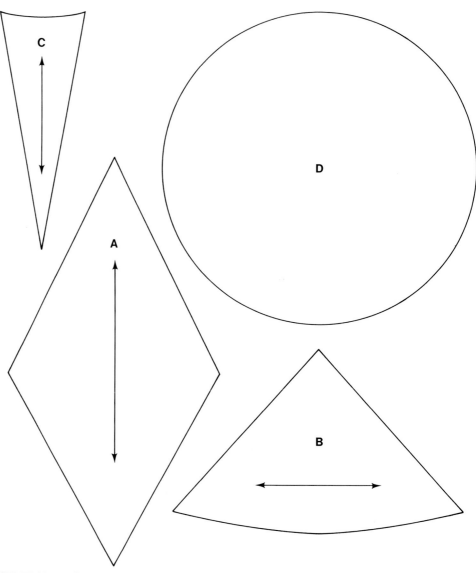

SUNFLOWER QUILT
Full-Size Patterns

pieces, draw around a template with
a pencil on the wrong side of the fabric; then, cut out the pieces, adding
¼-inch seam allowances.

CUTTING INSTRUCTIONS: From
background fabric, cut thirty 16-
inch squares. Squares can all be cut
from the same fabric. Or, to make a
quilt like the one shown on pages 92
and 93, cut squares from the varied

background fabrics listed in the materials list.

From the green print fabric, cut
360 A pieces.

From the yellow fabric, cut 360 C
pieces.

From assorted black and white
print and check fabrics, cut 360 B
pattern pieces.

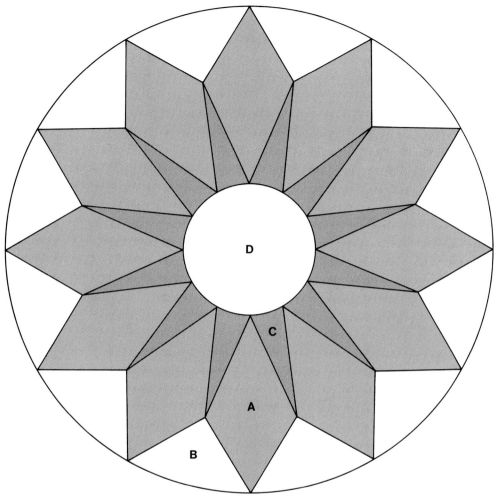

SUNFLOWER QUILT CIRCLE DIAGRAM

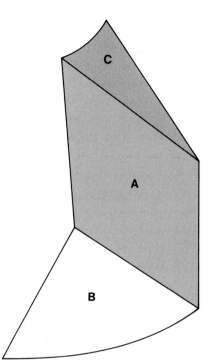

SUNFLOWER QUILT PIECING DIAGRAM

From the black and white pindotted fabric, cut 30 D circles.

TO MAKE ONE BLOCK: Referring to the piecing diagram, *above right,* sew a B piece and a C piece to an A piece. Repeat to make a total of 12 units. Stitch the units together to form a circle with an open center.

Baste under the seam allowances of a D circle. Appliqué the D circle over the opening to form the center of the sunflower.

Baste under the seam allowances around the outside of the sunflower circle. Appliqué the circle to the cen-

ter of a background square. Carefully trim away the portion of the background square under the circle, leaving approximately ¼-inch seam allowances.

Make 30 sunflower blocks.

TO SET THE QUILT TOP: Sew the quilt together in six horizontal rows with five blocks in each row. If you have chosen to use a variety of background squares, first lay out the blocks to determine a pleasing arrangement. Join the rows.

QUILT FINISHING INSTRUCTIONS: To piece the quilt back, cut or tear the backing fabric into two long panels. Split one fabric panel in half lengthwise. Taking ½-inch seam allowances and matching selvage edges, sew a half-panel to each side of the full panel. Trim off selvages so seam allowances are approximately ¼ inch. Press seams to one side.

Layer the quilt top, batting, and backing; baste. Quilt as desired, or follow these suggestions. Outline-quilt around the shapes in each block. Quilt a grid of ⅜-inch squares in the center of each sunflower. Quilt the background of each block in a grid of 1½-inch squares.

Cut approximately 10 yards of 2½-inch-wide binding from the binding fabric. Press the binding in half so it is 1¼ inches wide. Matching raw edges, stitch the binding to the quilt top. Trim batting and backing even with quilt top. Stitch the folded edge of the binding to the quilt back.

HIGH-COUNTRY SWEATERS

*The comfort, warmth, and style
of today's hand-knitted
outerwear is deeply rooted in the
traditional garments offered
here and on the following pages
of this chapter.*

Designed for rugged work or play, this man's drop-sleeve pullover features a Guernsey pattern—a check that is knitted with ribbing and garter stitches in a rich bulky tweed yarn.

The lady's pullover vest sports a sampler of duplicate-stitch designs that allows you to embellish as much or as little as you like. What a great way to use up some of your yarn remnants!

Instructions for knitting all sweaters and the hat in this chapter begin on page 112.

The festive Christmas tree on the lady's pullover, *opposite,* is knitted into the sweater. Small and large bobbles decorate the tree and form holly berries at the shoulders. You might even use the charted design on page 115 to work duplicate stitches on a purchased sweater.

The baby's cable cardigan and matching cap can be made to fit a child from six to 18 months. Cotton sport yarn gives the duo a nice, soft feel that baby will love. Raglan sleeves and a drawstring neck-line ensure that the sweater will fit any little figure. A row of single crochet supplies the nice crisp edging for the brim of the adorable bonnet.

The mountain weather may be nippy, but these snow lovers are as warm as toast in their wonderful knitted woolens.

The lady's textured jacket and hat, *opposite,* sport an allover pattern of horseshoe cables. A rolled ribbed collar can be worn up or down.

The matching boy's and girl's reindeer sweaters are knitted using the same pattern. Choose your favorite neckline—crew or turtleneck. You'll stitch the overall flecked pattern as you knit the body and sleeves, but work the reindeer and tree motifs separately using duplicate stitches.

Man's Guernsey Pullover

Shown on page 107.
Instructions are for Size Small.
Changes for Size Medium and
Size Large follow in parentheses.
Finished chest = 42 (46, 48)
inches.

MATERIALS
Tahki Soho Bulky Tweed (100-
gram skein): 9 (9, 10) skeins of
No. 393 yellow
Sizes 8 and 10½ knitting needles
or sizes to reach gauge given
below

Abbreviations: See page 187.
Gauge: With larger needles over st
st, 3 sts = 1 inch; 9 rows = 2
inches.

Stitches
GARTER-AND-RIB CHECK (see the
chart, *right*).

INSTRUCTIONS
BACK: With smaller needles, cast on
60 (62, 64) sts. Work in k 1, p 1 rib
for 3 inches, inc 6 (7, 8) sts evenly
spaced on last rib row—66 (69, 72)
sts. Change to larger needles and st
st and work even until total length
measures 14 inches; end with right-
side row. K 1 row, p 1 row, k 1 row.
Next row (right side): K 1 row, inc 4
(6, 8) sts evenly spaced across row by
forming backward lp on right needle—70 (75, 80) sts. P 1 row.
Beg Garter-and-Rib Check Pat,
working from chart, *right,* as follows:

For Sizes Small and Large
Right-side rows—Rep from A to B
across.
Wrong-side rows: Rep from B to A
across.

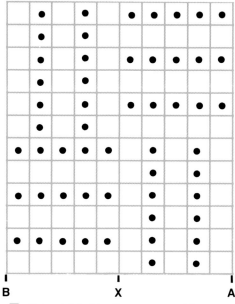

B   X   A

☐ K on right side, P on wrong side
▣ P on right side, K on wrong side
GARTER-AND-RIB CHECK PATTERN

For Size Medium
Right-side rows—Rep from A to B
across, ending at X.
Wrong-side rows: Beg at X, work
to A, rep from B to A across.
Continue in pat as established until total length measures 25 inches.

SHOULDER SHAPING: Bind off 8 (8,
9) sts at beg of next 4 rows, then
bind off 7 (8, 9) sts at beg of following
2 rows. Bind off rem 24 (27, 26) sts
for back neck.

FRONT: Work as for Back until total
length measures 22 inches, ending
with wrong-side row.

NECK SHAPING: Continuing in pat
as established, work across first 29
(31, 33) sts for left shoulder. Join
second ball of yarn and bind off cen-

ter 12 (13, 14) sts. Complete row in
pat—29 (31, 33) sts each side. Working both sides at once, dec 1 st each
neck edge every other row 6 (7, 6)
times—23 (24, 27) sts each side.

SHOULDER SHAPING: Bind off at
shoulder edges every other row 8 (8,
9) sts twice, then 7 (8, 9) sts once.

SLEEVES: With smaller needles,
cast on 26 (28, 28) sts and work k 1,
p 1 ribbing for 3 inches, inc 12 sts
evenly spaced—38 (40, 40) sts.
Change to larger needles and st st,
inc 1 st at each end of needle every
fourth (fourth, third) row 11 (13, 15)
times—60 (66, 70) sts. Work even
until sleeve measures 15½ (16,
16½) inches, ending with right-side
row. K 1 row, p 1 row, k 1 row.
Next row (right side): K, inc 5 (4, 5)
sts evenly spaced across row by
forming backward lp on right needle—65 (70, 75) sts.
Next row: Purl. Beg Garter-and-
Rib Check Pat, working from chart
on page 99 as follows:

For Sizes Small and Large
Right-side rows—Rep from A to B
across, ending at X.
Wrong-side rows: Beg at X, work
to A, rep from B to A across.

For Size Medium
Right-side rows—Rep from A to B
across.
Wrong-side rows: Rep from B to A
across.
Continue in pat until total length
measures 19½ (20, 20½) inches.
Bind off all sts.

FINISHING: Seam right shoulder.
With smaller needles, pick up and k
54 (56, 58) sts around neck edge.
Work k 1, p 1 ribbing for 1¼ inches;
bind off in rib. Seam left shoulder.
Sew sleeve to body across patterned
area of yoke. Sew side and sleeve
seams.

Sampler Vest

Shown on pages 106 and 107. Instructions are for Size Small. Changes for Size Medium and Size Large follow in parentheses.

MATERIALS
8 ounces of gray worsted-weight yarn
Remnant worsted-weight yarn in the colors of your choice or in colors listed: black, off-white, gray, medium forest green, dark blue, white, and brown
Sizes 7 and 8 knitting needles

Abbreviations: See page 187.
Gauge: 11 stitches and 13 rows = 2 inches on Size 8 needles.

INSTRUCTIONS
STRIPE PATTERN: Working in the stockinette stitch (k 1 row, p 1 row), work rows as follows:
  14 rows off-white
  2 rows black
  11 rows medium forest green
  2 rows black
  10 rows dark blue
  2 rows black
  10 rows white
  2 rows black
  8 rows gray
  2 rows black
  8 rows brown
  2 rows black
  16 rows dark blue
  2 rows black
  8 rows off-white
  2 rows black
  Continue to knit with gray until all shaping is complete.

BACK: With Size 7 needles and gray cast on 75 (79, 83) stitches and work in k 1, p 1 ribbing for 2½ inches. Change to the Size 8 needles and *continued*

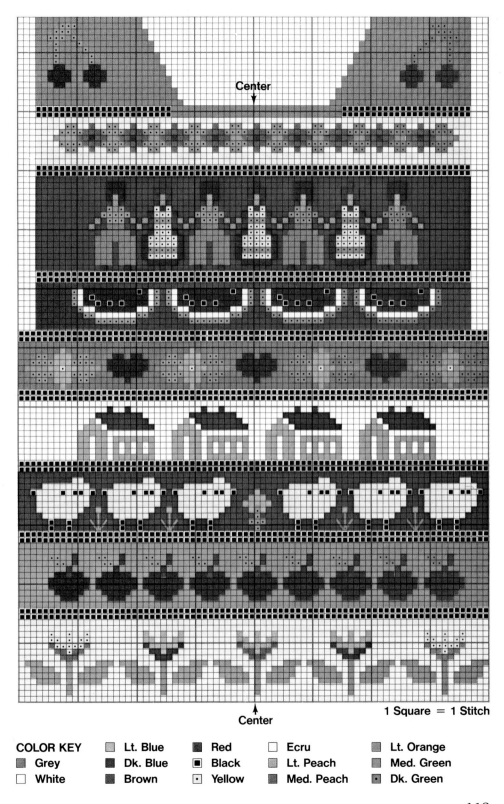

Center

Center

1 Square = 1 Stitch

COLOR KEY

☐ Lt. Blue	◼ Red	☐ Ecru	▨ Lt. Orange
◼ Grey	◼ Dk. Blue	◼ Black	☐ Lt. Peach	▨ Med. Green
☐ White	◼ Brown	⊡ Yellow	◼ Med. Peach	⊡ Dk. Green

work in st st increasing 5 sts evenly spaced across first row—80 (84, 88) sts. Work until piece is 14 (15, 16) inches from beginning, ending with a purl row.

SHAPE ARMHOLES: Cast off 3 (5, 7) stitches at the beginning of next 2 rows. Continue working until armholes measure 6½ (7, 7½) inches. With right side facing, bind off 14 (16, 18) stitches. Work across 46 (42, 48) stitches. Bind off remaining 14 (16, 18) stitches. Place remaining stitches on holder for back neck.

FRONT: Work in stripe pattern following directions for Back until armholes measure 2½ (3, 3½) inches.

NECK SHAPING: Work across 23 (21, 19) stitches, k 2 tog, k 1, turn, purl back across only one shoulder. Continue to decrease 1 stitch at neck edge as established every row until 14 (16, 18) stitches remain. Work on these stitches continuing in stripe pattern until armhole measures same as back. Bind off one shoulder. Place center 22 (26, 30) stitches on holder and with right side of work facing finish the second side. Decrease 1 stitch at neck edge every row as follows: K 1, sl 1, k1, psso, knit to end of row. Purl next row. Continue in this manner until 14 (16, 18) stitches remain. Work until second armhole measures same as back. With knit side facing, bind off.

FINISHING: Sew left shoulder seam. With right side facing and gray, pick up and knit 92 (98, 104) stitches around neck including those stitches on holders. Work in k 1, p 1 ribbing for ¾ inch. Bind off in rib. Sew right shoulder seam. With right side facing pick up and knit 68 (72, 76) stitches around armholes. Work in k 1, p 1 ribbing for ¾ inch. Bind off. Sew side seams.

Embroider designs on sweater front using duplicate stitches and following pattern on page 113. Center design and work toward the sides.

Christmas Tree Pullover

Shown on page 108.
Directions are for Size Small. Changes for Size Medium and Size Large follow in parentheses. Finished bust = 37 (39½, 43) inches.

MATERIALS
Manos del Uruguay (4-ounce skein): 4 (5, 6) skeins of red; one skein *each* of blue, pale gold, and green
Sizes 6 and 9 knitting needles or size to reach gauge given below

Abbreviations: See page 187.
Gauge: With larger needles over charted pattern 9 sts = 2 inches; 5 rows = 1 inch.

Stitches
SMALL BOBBLE: K in front and back of next st, turn; p 2, turn; k 2 tog.

LARGE BOBBLE: (K in front and back of st) twice, turn; p 4, turn; k 4, turn; p 4, turn; sl second, third, and fourth st over first st.

INSTRUCTIONS
FRONT: With smaller needles and red, cast on 71 (75, 79) sts.

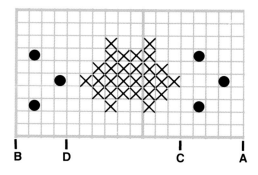

1 Square = 1 Stitch

CHART 1
COLOR KEY
● French Knot, Red
⊠ Green
☐ Pale Gold

Work in k 1, p 1 ribbing for 3 inches, inc 12 (14, 18) sts evenly spaced on last rib row—83 (89, 97) sts.

Change to larger needles, st st and blue; work 2 rows. Beg Chart 1, *above,* as follows: (*Note:* Holly berries of Chart 1 are worked in French knots with red when garment is finished. They are included on the chart to indicate position only.)

Size Small: Beg at A, work to B; rep from C to B across.

Size Medium: Work 3 sts with red, place marker, work chart as for Size Small (3 sts rem unworked), place marker, work last 3 sts in red.

Size Large: Work from A to B; rep from C to B across (1 st rem unworked); work last st in red.

All sizes: Continue working from chart as established, working 3 extra stitches sizes Medium and Large in red. When Chart 1 is completed, work 2 rows blue, then work 2 (4, 6) rows red.

Begin Chart 2, *opposite,* as follows: (*Note:* Work large and small bobbles in contrasting colors at random on tree motif as desired; work

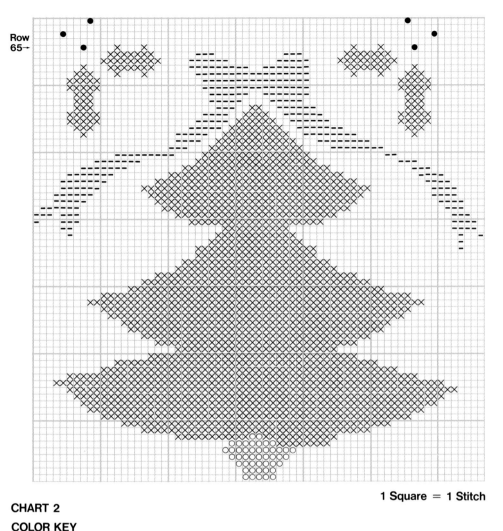

Row 65→

1 Square = 1 Stitch

CHART 2

COLOR KEY

⊠ Green ⊟ Blue ⊙ Pale Gold ● Red Bobble ☐ Red

the bobbles for the holly berries as indicated on Chart 2). K 8 (11, 15) red, work Row 1 of Chart 2 over center 67 sts, complete row with red. Continue working from chart as established, keeping sts at each side of chart in red and working even until total length measures 14½ (15, 15) inches.

ARMHOLE SHAPING: Keeping to pat, bind off 4 sts at beg of next 2 rows, 2 sts at beg of next 4 rows; dec 1 st each side every other row 3 times—61 (67, 75) sts. Work even until Row 65 of chart is complete.

NECK SHAPING: Keeping to pat, work 23 (25, 27) sts, join second ball

of yarn and bind off center 15 (17, 21) sts for front neck, complete row. Working both sides at the same time, bind off at each neck edge 3 sts once, then 2 sts once. Dec 1 st 4 times—14 (16, 18) sts. Work even until length from beg of armhole shaping measures 7½ (8, 8½) inches. At the same time, when all chart rows have been worked, continue with red only.

SHOULDER SHAPING: At each armhole edge bind off 4 sts 2 (0, 0) times, 5 sts 0 (2, 0) times, 6 sts 1 (1, 3) times.

BACK: Work as for Front until 2 rows of blue are completed after Chart 1. Complete to correspond to Front with red, except do not work from chart.

SLEEVES: With smaller needles and red, cast on 34 (36, 38) sts. Work in k 1, p 1 ribbing for 3 inches, inc 6 (4, 2) sts evenly spaced on last rib row—40 sts.

Change to larger needles, st st and blue; work 2 rows. Work Chart 1 as follows: Beg at A and work to B, rep from C to B once, then work from C to D. Continue working from chart as established until chart is completed. Work 2 rows blue. Complete sleeve with red as follows: inc 1 st each end of next row, then every sixth row 7 (8, 9) times more—56 (58, 60) sts. Work even until total length measures 16½ (17, 17½) inches.

TOP SHAPING: Bind off 4 sts at beg of next 2 rows, then 2 sts at beg of next 4 rows. Dec 1 st each end every row 8 times, then dec 1 st each end every other row 3 (4, 5) times. Bind off 3 sts at beg of next 6 rows.

continued

FINISHING: Sew the right shoulder seam of the sweater.

NECKBAND: With smaller needles, red, and with right side facing and beg at left front neck edge, pick up 76 (80, 84) sts evenly spaced along entire neck edge. Work in k 1, p 1 ribbing for 1 inch. Bind off in ribbing. Sew left shoulder and neckband seam. Sew side and sleeve seams. Set in sleeves.

With red, work French knots for holly berries as indicated on charts on pages 114 and 115, adjusting placement at side seams to continue pat across the seams.

Baby's Cable Cardigan and Cap

Shown on page 109.
Directions are for Size 6 Months.
Changes for Sizes 1 Year and 18 Months follow in parentheses.

MATERIALS
Coats and Clark Red Heart 100% Cotton Sport Yarn, Art. E. 284: 7 (7, 8) ounces of No. 850 Blueberry
Sizes 4 and 6 knitting needles
Five ½-inch-diameter buttons
Cable needle
Size F crochet hook

Abbreviations: See page 187.
Gauge: On Size 6 needles in st st, 6 sts = 1 inch; 15 rows = 2 inches. Be sure to check your gauge. Use any size needles that will obtain the gauge given.

INSTRUCTIONS
Use the following measurements when deciding which size to make:

Body/Chest Size: 19 (20, 21) inches
Width across back at underarm: 10 (10½, 11) inches
Width across each front at underarm: 5¼ (5½, 5¾) inches
Length of side seam: 6½ (7, 7½) inches
Length of sleeve seam: 7 (7½, 8) inches
Width across sleeve at upper arm: 7 (7¼, 7½) inches

BACK: With Size 4 needles, cast on 56 (60, 64) sts. Work in k 1, p 1 ribbing for 7 (7, 9) rows. Change to Size 6 needles and work in st st until piece measures 6½ (7, 7½) inches in all. Bind off 3 sts at beg of next 2 rows.
Next row: K 2, k 2 tog, k to last 4 sts, sl 1, k 1, psso, k 2.
Next row: Purl. Rep these 2 rows until 24 sts rem. Place these sts on holder.

LEFT FRONT: With Size 4 needle, cast on 34 (36, 38) sts.
Row 1: K 1, p 1, for 5 (5, 7) sts, place a marker on the needle, k 1, p 1 to end.
Row 2: Work in ribbing to marker, k 1, p 1 to end (seed st border). Rep these 2 rows 2 (2, 3) times more; then rep Row 1.
Change to Size 6 needle.
Row 1: K 12 (13, 13) sts, p 2, k 6, p 2, k 7 (8, 8), work 5 (5, 7) seed sts.
Row 2: Work 5 (5, 7) seed sts, p 7 (8, 8), k 2, p 6, k 2, p to end.
Row 3: K 12 (13, 13) sts, p 2, slip next 3 sts to cable needle and hold in back, k next 3 sts, k 3 from cable needle, p 2, k to end.
Rows 4 and 6: Rep Row 2.
Row 5: Rep Row 1. Rep these 6 rows for pat until piece measures same as back to underarm. End at

arm edge. Continuing in pat, bind off 3 sts at beg of next row; then dec 1 st at arm edge as on back every other row until 25 (25, 26) sts rem; end at arm edge.

NECK SHAPING: Continuing to dec at arm edge, place center 12 sts on a holder; then dec 1 st at neck edge every row 4 times. Continue to dec at arm edge until 2 sts rem. Place on a holder. Mark seed st band for five buttons having the first at Row 4 and the last at top of band.

RIGHT FRONT: Work same as Left Front, reversing all shaping. Make buttonhole on seed st band on Row 4 as follows: 2 (2, 3) seed st, yo, k 2 tog, work 2 (2, 3) seed st. Work 4 more buttonholes opposite button marks. Sew side and sleeve seams.

NECK: With Size 4 needles, pick up 80 sts around entire neck, including sts on holders. Work in k 1, p 1 ribbing for 2¼ inches; bind off loosely in ribbing. Fold ribbing to inside and sew in place. Using a double strand of yarn and crochet hook, work a ch about 30 inches long and thread through neck band.

TASSELS: Wind yarn around 3 fingers about 30 times, tie through center and attach to end of chain. Tie yarn tightly at top of tassel. Trim lower end. Sew on buttons.

HAT: With Size 4 needles, cast on 77 sts and work in k 1, p 1 ribbing for 6 rows (front). Change to Size 6 needles and k 1 row (wrong side); mark this row.

PATTERN: *Row 1:* * K 19, p 2, k 6, p 2; rep from * once, k 19.
Row 2: * p 19, k 2, p 6, k 2; rep from * once, k 19.

Rows 3 and 4: Rep rows 1 and 2.

Row 5: * K 19, p 2, sl next 3 sts to cable needle and hold in back, k next 3 sts, k 3 from cable needle, p 2; rep from * once, k 19.

Row 6: Rep Row 2. Rep these 6 rows for pat until piece measures 4 inches from top of ribbing, end with an even row. Bind off 27 sts at beg of next 2 rows. Work in st st on rem 23 sts for back flap; dec 1 st each side every 6th row until 15 sts rem. Work even until flap measures 4½ inches. Bind off. Sew sides of flap to the 27 bound-off sts on each side.

With right side facing, and Size 4 needles, and starting at edge of front ribbing, pick up 18 sts along left side, 15 sts along back flap and 18 sts along right side, ending at other edge of front ribbing (51 sts). Work in k1, p 1 ribbing for 5 rows. Bind off.

BRIM: With Size 4 needles, right side facing, and starting on left side on marked row, pick up and k 77 sts of marked row. P 1 row.

Next row: * K 2, inc 1 in next st; rep from * across, end k 2—102 sts. P 1 row. Working in st st, dec 1 st each side every row 12 times—78 sts. P 1 row on right side—turning row.

Next row: P; inc 1 st each side. Working in st st, inc 1 st each side 11 times more—102 sts. P 1 row.

Next row: * K 2, k 2 tog; rep from * across, end k 2—77 sts. P 1 row; bind off. Fold in half with wrong sides together and sew in place. With crochet hook work 1 row of sc through both thicknesses on sides and along turning row. Using a double strand of yarn crochet a chain about 7 inches long and attach to front edge of back ribbing. Make tassels as for sweater, winding yarn about 16 times.

Lopi Textured Hat

Shown on page 111.
One size fits all.

MATERIALS

Reynolds Lopi (100-gram skein): 1 skein of No. 051 natural
Sizes 9 and 10½ knitting needles or size to reach gauge given below
Double-pointed needle (dpn)

Abbreviations: See page 187.
Gauge: With larger needles over st st, 3 sts = 1 inch.

Stitches

CABLE PATTERN: *Row 1 (wrong side) and all other wrong-side rows through Row 7:* Purl.

Row 2: K 1, * sl 3 to dpn and hold in back of work, k 3, k 3 from dpn, sl 3 to dpn and hold in front of work, k 3, k 3 from dpn; rep from *, end k 1.

Rows 4, 6, and 8: Knit. Rep rows 1–8 for pat.

INSTRUCTIONS

With smaller needles cast on 72 sts. Work in k 1, p 1 rib for 3 inches, inc 2 sts in last row and ending with right-side row—74 sts. Change to larger needles and work in Cable Pat until total length measures 7 inches, dec 2 sts in last row and ending with wrong-side row—72 sts.

SHAPE TOP: Change to st st.

Row 1: * K 4, k 2 tog; rep from * across—60 sts.

Row 2 and all wrong-side rows: Purl.

Row 3: * K 3, k 2 tog; rep from * across—48 sts.

Row 5: * K 2, k 2 tog; rep from * across—36 sts.

Row 7: * K 1, k 2 tog; rep from * across—24 sts.

Rows 9 and 11: K 2 tog across—6 sts at end of Row 11. Break off yarn, leaving 18-inch tail. With tapestry needle, draw wool through rem 6 sts and pull tightly. Sew back seam.

Lopi Textured Jacket

Shown on page 111.
Directions are for Size Small/Medium. Changes for Size Medium/Large follow in parentheses. Finished bust = 40 (44) inches.

MATERIALS

Reynolds Lopi (100-gram skein): 11 (14) skeins of No. 051 natural
Sizes 9 and 10½ knitting needles or size to reach gauge given below
Double-pointed needle (dpn)
Eight ⅞-inch-diameter buttons

Abbreviations: See page 187.
Gauge: With larger needles over st st, 3 sts = 1 inch.

Stitches

CABLE PATTERN: *Row 1 (wrong side) and all other wrong-side rows through Row 7:* Purl.

Row 2: K 1, * sl 3 to dpn and hold in back of work, k 3, k 3 from dpn, sl 3 to dpn and hold in front of work, k 3, k 3 from dpn; rep from *, end k 1.

Rows 4, 6, and 8: Knit. Rep rows 1–8 for pat.

INSTRUCTIONS

BACK: With smaller needles, cast on 84 (96) sts. Work in k 1, p 1 rib for 2½ inches, inc 14 sts evenly spaced in last row and ending with right-side row—98 (110) sts.

continued

Change to larger needles and pat st, working even until total length measures 26 (27) inches. Bind off 34 (38) sts. Sl st rem on right needle to holder, sl next 29 (33) sts to same holder for back of neck; bind off rem 34 (38) sts.

LEFT FRONT: With smaller needles cast on 44 (48) sts.

Work in k 1, p 1 rib for 2½ inches, inc 6 sts on last row and ending with right-side row—50 (54) sts.

Change to larger needles and beg Cable Pat as follows: P 0 (2), work Row 1 of Cable Pat over center 50 sts, p last 0 (2) sts. Keeping to Cable Pat as established and keeping sts outside of Cable Pat on Medium/Large in st st as established, work even until total length measures 22 (23) inches, ending at center front opening edge.

NECK SHAPING: Work first 12 sts in pat and sl to holder for front neck; complete row in pat.

Keeping to pat, dec 1 st at neck edge every other row 4 times—34 (38) sts. Work even until total length measures 26 (27) inches. Bind off all of the sts.

RIGHT FRONT: Work as for Left Front, reversing neck shaping.

SLEEVES: With smaller needles cast on 34 (36) sts.

Work in k 1, p 1 rib for 3 inches, inc 28 (26) sts evenly spaced in last row and ending with right-side row—62 (62) sts.

Change to larger needles, work in Cable Pat for rem of sleeve. At the same time, inc 1 st each end every 1½ (1⅛) inches 10 (12) times, working new sts in st st—82 (86) sts. Work even until total length measures 19 (20) inches. Bind off all sts.

Sew shoulder seams.

NECKBAND: With smaller needles, and beg at right neck edge, work across 12 sts from front neck holder, pick up and k 17 sts along right neck edge, work 30 (34) sts from back neck holder, pick up and k 17 sts along left neck edge, work across 12 sts from front neck holder—88 (92) sts.

Work in k 1, p 1 rib for 6 inches. Bind off using larger needles.

LEFT FRONT BAND: Fold neckband in half to outside.

With right side facing, smaller needles, and working on left front edge, pick up and k 11 sts through both thicknesses of neckband, then pick up and k 79 (85) sts to lower edge—90 (96) sts.

Work in k 1, p 1 rib for 1 inch. Bind off loosely in rib.

RIGHT FRONT BAND: Beg at lower right front edge, with right side facing, and with smaller needles, pick up and k 90 (96) sts along right front edge.

Work in k 1, p 1 rib for ½ inch, ending with wrong-side row.

Next row: Rib first 4 sts, [bind off 2 sts, work in rib over next 11 (12) sts] 6 times, (bind off 2 sts, work in rib over 2 sts) twice.

Following row: Working in rib, cast on 2 sts over bound-off sts of previous row to complete buttonholes.

Work even in rib until total width of band measures 1 inch. Bind off all sts loosely in rib.

FINISHING: Place markers at armhole edge of Front and Back 10 (11) inches below shoulder seams.

Set in sleeves between markers. Sew side and sleeve seams. Sew buttons opposite the buttonholes.

Child's Reindeer Pullover

Shown on pages 110 and 111. Directions are for child's Size 12; changes for Sizes 14 and 16 follow in parentheses. Chest = 31½ (33, 35½) inches.

MATERIALS
Unger Skol (1.6-ounce ball): 7 (7, 8) balls natural (MC), 1 ball dark green (A), and 1 ball wine (B)
Sizes 8 and 10 knitting needles, or size to obtain gauge given below
Tapestry needle

Abbreviations: See page 187.
Gauge: With larger needles over st st, 7 sts = 2 inches; 5 rows = 1 inch.

INSTRUCTIONS
Note: Twist yarns on wrong side when working with 2 colors to prevent making holes. Carry color not in use loosely across back, being careful to maintain gauge. Reindeer and tree added later in duplicate st when pieces are completed.

BACK: With smaller needles and MC, cast on 57 (59, 63) sts. Work k 1, p 1 ribbing for 2½ inches. Change to larger needles and st st. Work 2 rows even. Now beg pat as follows:

Row 1 (right side): K 4 (5, 7) MC, k 1 A, * k 7 MC, k 1 A. Rep from * across, ending with k 4 (5, 7) MC.

Rows 2, 4, and 6: With MC, p.
Rows 3 and 5: With MC, k.
Row 7: K 8 (1, 3) MC, k 1 A, * k 7 MC, k 1 A. Rep from * across, ending with k 8 (1, 3) MC.

Rows 8, 10, and 12: With MC, p.
Rows 9 and 11: With MC, k. Rep these 12 rows from pat. Work even until the 4th time row 8 (10, 12) has been completed.

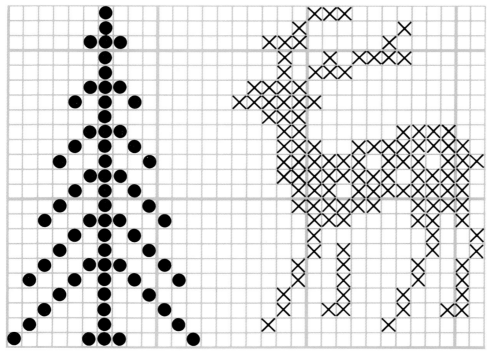

COLOR KEY ● Dark Green (A) ☒ Wine (B)   1 Square = 1 Stitch

YOKE: *Row 1* (right side): K 1 MC, * k 1 A, k 1 MC. Rep from * across.

Row 2: P 2 MC, p 1 A, * p 1 MC, p 1 A. Rep from * across ending with p 2 MC. Fasten off A. With MC only, work 26 (26, 28) rows even in st st. *Note:* This MC panel is where duplicate st reindeer and tree will be worked.

* Rep rows 1 and 2 of yoke pat, work 2 rows even with MC. Rep from * until there are 10 (12, 14) rows in all above end of MC panel.

SHOULDER SHAPING: With MC only, bind off 18 (19, 20) sts, k 21 (21, 23) sts and sl these sts onto a holder for back of neck, bind off rem 18 (19, 20) sts.

FRONT: Work as for Back until work is 12 (12, 14) rows less to shoulders than back—57 (59, 63) sts.

NECK SHAPING: Keeping to pat, work 23 (24, 25) sts. Sl rem sts to holder. Working on left side only, dec 1 st at neck edge every row 3 times, then every other row twice—18 (19, 20) sts. Work to shoulder as for Back. Bind off. Leaving center 9 (11, 13) sts on holder, sl rem 23 (24, 25) sts onto needle. Attach yarn at neck edge and work to correspond to other side, reversing shaping.

Neckband for crew neck
Sew left shoulder seam. With MC, smaller needles, and right side facing, pick up 61 (63, 65) sts around neck, including sts on holders. Work k 1, p 1 ribbing for 2¼ inches. Bind off loosely in ribbing.

Neckband for turtleneck
Work even in ribbing for 5 (5½, 6) inches. Fold crew neckband in half to inside; sew loosely in place.

SLEEVES: Along side edges, measure down 6½ (7, 7½) inches from shoulder seams and place a marker at back and front. With larger needles, MC, and right side facing, pick up 45 (49, 51) sts along armhole edge, from marker to marker. Beg with a p row and work even in st st for 4 rows. Dec 1 st at each end of next row—43 (47, 49) sts. Work 1 row even and beg pat as follows:

Row 1: With MC, k 1 (3, 4), k 1 A, * k 7 MC, k 1 A. Rep from * across, ending with k 1 (3, 4) MC.

Row 2: With MC, p.

Row 3: With MC, k and dec 1 st each end—41 (45, 47) sts.

Rows 4 and 6: Rep Row 2.

Row 5: With MC, k.

Row 7: K 4 (6, 7) MC, k 1 A, * k 7 MC, k 1 A. Rep from * across, ending with k 4 (6, 7). Continue in pat as established, dec 1 st each end every 10th row 5 times more and adjusting pat for the decs—31 (35, 37) sts. Work even to total of 13 (14, 15) inches or 3 inches less than desired length, ending on wrong side.

Change to smaller needles and MC. *Row 1:* K across, dec 8 (10, 10) sts evenly spaced—23 (25, 27) sts. Work in k 1, p 1 ribbing for 3 in. Bind off loosely in ribbing.

PATTERN FOR WORKING DUPLICATE STITCHES: Mark center st of front and back in the 2nd (2nd, 3rd) row of MC panel and work tree in duplicate st (see diagram, *above*) on center of front and back.

Beg in 3rd (3rd, 4th) row of MC panel, and work left reindeer in duplicate st on front and back. Reverse pat and work right reindeer in duplicate st on front and back.

FINISHING: Weave ends. Sew under sleeve and side seams. Block on wrong side to measurements.

THE SPIRIT OF AMERICAN CHRISTMAS

*Hooray for the red, white, and blue!
This collection of lively
Christmas trims is tailor-made for
those who delight in handmade things
that project a patriotic spirit.*

A glow with the colors of Old Glory, this all-American tree, *right,* is brimming with patriotic trims you can craft with pride.

Miniature American flags of hand-painted muslin are tucked between the tree's branches along with larger store-bought flags. Tea-dye the cotton flags for an antique look.

Painted pine soldier and Uncle Sam ornaments have movable arms and legs and can sit on branches, cross their legs, hold flags, and be placed in a variety of other poses.

Small wooden drums are made with 1½-inch-diameter dowel cut into 2-inch lengths. Paint them with stars and stripes, and add a loop of twine to hang the ornament.

For information on other projects, please turn the page.

Instructions begin on page 124.

THE SPIRIT OF AMERICAN CHRISTMAS

With his woolly white beard and smartly striped top hat, Uncle Sam is certainly among America's most renowned political symbols.

Invite the 18-inch Sam doll, *opposite,* to preside at your holiday festivities. This painted pine figure has movable arms and legs, so he can sit as easily upon a mantel as he can beneath your tree.

Stars and stripes decorate the painted drum boxes, *opposite* and on pages 120 and 121.

To make these distinctive catchalls, purchase wooden band or cheese boxes in various sizes and embellish them with acrylics.

Paint pieces of driftwood to create the firecrackers, *opposite.* Use these little sparklers to add interest to a wreath, mantel, or table display.

Toy soldiers march gallantly across the boy's pullover, *left.* Knit the sweater with sport-weight yarn, then embroider the soldiers and sleeve stripes with duplicate stitches.

Drum Ornaments

Shown on pages 120 and 121.
Finished drums are 1½ inches
in diameter and 2 inches high.

MATERIALS
1½-inch-diameter wooden dowel
Sandpaper
Woodworking saw
Ivory, barn-red, and blue acrylic
   paint
Artist's brushes
Toothpicks
Antiquing glaze
Drill with ¼-inch drill bit
Twine
Old rags for glazing
Crafts glue

INSTRUCTIONS
Cut 1½-inch dowel into 2-inch
lengths. Sand all rough surfaces.
   Paint all surfaces of each dowel
section with a base coat of ivory
paint. Allow the paint to dry.
   Using a ¼-inch drill bit, drill a hole
¼ inch deep in the center of the top
of each drum.
   Evenly paint barn-red stripes
around the entire outside of each
drum. Paint a ¼-inch-wide blue
band at the top and the bottom of
each drum. Use a toothpick dipped
in ivory paint to paint stars on top of
the blue bands. (Refer to the photograph on pages 120 and 121 for
guidance.) Allow each paint color to
dry before applying the next.
   Using an old rag, wipe a thin coat
of antiquing stain over all surfaces of
each drum. Allow the stain to set a
few minutes, then wipe excess away.
   Cut twine into 8-inch lengths.
Glue ends in hole in top of each
drum. Allow glue to dry thoroughly
before hanging.

Muslin Flags

Shown on pages 120 and 121.

MATERIALS
Unbleached muslin
¼-inch dowel
Ivory, barn-red, and blue fabric
   paint
Artist's brushes
Toothpicks
Instant tea
Crafts glue

INSTRUCTIONS
Note: Instructions are given for making your own flags. You can purchase small flags and tea-dye them
following the directions for finishing
the flags, *below.*

TO MAKE THE FLAGS: Cut one 3x4-
inch piece of muslin for each flag ornament. Draw stripes and the star
area on the pieces of muslin.
   Paint the stripes red and the field
for the stars blue. Use a toothpick to
paint the ivory stars on the blue field.
Allow each color of paint to dry before going on to the next.
   Cut a 10-inch length of dowel.
Glue the left side of the flag to the
wooden dowel.

FINISHING: Mix a strong solution of
instant tea and a small amount of
water. Dip each flag in the tea until
the flag is wet.
   Hold the flag by the dowel and pull
it downward to shape. (See the photograph on pages 120 and 121.)
   Lay the flags flat to dry.

Firecrackers

Shown on pages 120–122.

MATERIALS
Assorted sizes of driftwood
Ivory, barn-red, and blue acrylic
   paints
Artist's brushes
Drill with ¼-inch drill bit
Twine
Antiquing glaze

INSTRUCTIONS
Select lengths of driftwood that are
reasonably straight. Choose a variety
of thicknesses so you can make all
sizes of firecrackers. Cut the driftwood to desired lengths, depending
upon the diameter of the wood.
   Refer to the photograph on page
122 for painting. Base-coat each firecracker with ivory, red, or blue acrylic. Paint stars, stripes, and bands of
color using artist's brushes and
acrylic paints. Allow paint to dry before applying the next color.
   Drill a hole ¼ inch deep in the top
of each firecracker. Cut a 2-inch
length of twine. Glue the twine
"fuse" in place in the hole. Allow the
glue to dry.

Chunky Wooden Heart

Shown on pages 120–122.
Finished size is 5x8 inches.

MATERIALS
12 inches of 4x6-inch fir
Red, white, and blue acrylic paint
Sandpaper
Band saw

INSTRUCTIONS
Sketch a 5x8-inch heart on fir. Cut
out the shape with a band saw.
Lightly sand rough edges.

Referring to the photograph on page 122, paint the flag design on heart. When all paint is dry, lightly sand edge and random areas to make the heart look worn.

Drum Boxes

Shown on pages 120–122.

MATERIALS
Purchased wooden band or cheese boxes in graduated sizes
Ivory, barn-red, blue, and gold acrylic paints
Artist's brushes
1-inch-wide paintbrush
Antiquing glaze

INSTRUCTIONS
Apply a base coat of ivory acrylic paint over all surfaces of each box. Allow the paint to dry.

Lightly draw an even number of stripes, evenly spaced, around the box. Paint the alternating stripes barn red. Paint a blue band at the bottom of each box and around the edge of the lid.

Use an artist's brush and gold acrylic to paint stars on top of the blue bands. (Refer to the photograph on page 122 for guidance.) Allow each paint color to dry before applying the next.

Using an old rag, wipe a thin coat of antiquing stain over all surfaces of each box. Allow the stain to set a few minutes, then wipe excess away.

Jointed Soldier And Uncle Sam Ornaments

Shown on pages 120–122. Finished size of each ornament is 6½ inches tall.

MATERIALS
Scraps of ¾-inch pine (body, head, arms, legs, and hat brim)
1-inch length of ⅝-inch dowel (Uncle Sam's hat)
1-inch-diameter circle of ½-inch pine (hat brim)
½ inch of ¼-inch-diameter dowel
Drill with ⅝- and ¼-inch drill bits
Saw
Sandpaper
Twine
Ivory, barn-red, flesh, blue, gold, and black acrylic paints
Artist's brushes
Antiquing glaze
Natural wool or cotton (hair), or substitute polyester fiberfill
Crafts glue

INSTRUCTIONS
For the ornaments
The patterns, *right,* are full size. The body, arm, and leg pieces are the same for the soldier and Uncle Sam. Only the head piece is different.

Refer to the directions for the Uncle Sam jointed doll on page 126 for construction of the jointed ornaments, noting the following changes for the head assembly and the special instructions for the soldiers:

The heads of the ornaments are glued, not doweled, to the bodies.

The soldier's head and hat are cut from one piece of wood. His hair and mustache are painted on the head with black acrylic paint. His buttons and the trim on his hat are gold.

A ¼-inch deep hole is drilled in the hat top, and a loop of twine is glued in place for hanging the ornament.

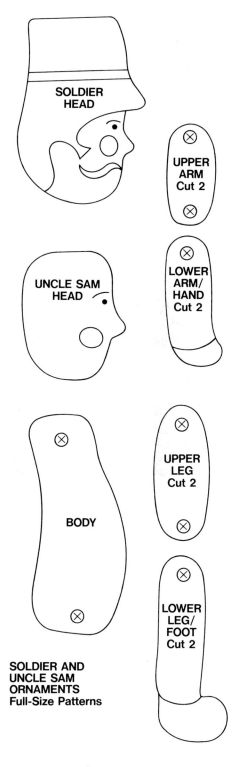

SOLDIER HEAD

UNCLE SAM HEAD

UPPER ARM Cut 2

LOWER ARM/ HAND Cut 2

BODY

UPPER LEG Cut 2

LOWER LEG/ FOOT Cut 2

SOLDIER AND UNCLE SAM ORNAMENTS Full-Size Patterns

Uncle Sam Jointed Doll

Shown on pages 120–122.
Finished size is 18 inches tall.

MATERIALS
1½-inch pine (body, head)
½-inch pine (arms, legs, hat brim)
2¼-inch length of 1½-inch-
  diameter dowel (hat)
1½ inches of ¼-inch-diameter
  dowel
Drill with ⅛- and ¼-inch drill bits
Woodworker's carving knife
Saw
Sandpaper
Twine
Ivory, barn-red, flesh, blue, and
  black acrylic paint
Artist's brushes
Antiquing glaze
Natural wool or cotton (hair), or
  substitute polyester fiberfill
Crafts glue

INSTRUCTIONS
For the doll
Using the full-size pattern pieces, *opposite*, cut out head, body, arms, and legs/feet from the appropriate pieces of wood. Sand all edges smooth.

FOR THE HEAD: From the side view of the head pattern piece, you can easily see the nose shape. Turn the face surface toward you. Using a woodworker's carving knife, carve away the wood on each side of the nose, leaving a nose shape approximately ⅜ inch wide. Shape the nose, referring to the photograph on page 122 as a guide.

Carve away part of the bottom of the head to form a lower jawline.

PAINTING THE PIECES: Using the acrylic paints, base-coat the head flesh color, the body and arms blue, and the leg pieces ivory.

Paint the lower part of the arm (hand area) flesh. Paint the shoes black; add red stripes to the leg pieces. Using ivory, make small button dots down the front of the body.

Paint red cheeks, ivory eyebrows, and black eyes with ivory pupils on the face. (Refer to the photograph on page 122 and the face pattern on page 125 for features.)

Rub antiquing glaze over all shapes. Allow glaze to set for a few minutes. Wipe away excess glaze with an old cloth.

JOINING THE PIECES: Drill a ¼-inch-diameter hole ¼ inch deep in the top of the body and the bottom of the head. Cut a 1½-inch length of ¼-inch-diameter dowel. Glue one end of the dowel in the bottom of the head. The other end rests, but is not glued, in the hole in the top of the body. This allows the head to turn freely in place.

Drill ⅛-inch-diameter holes completely through the side of the body, at top for arm placement and bottom for leg placement, and through the arms and the legs as indicated by the Xs on the pattern pieces. Run a 10-inch length of twine through each of the holes in the body, leaving an equal amount of twine showing on both sides. Set the body aside.

Join upper and lower arms by threading twine through the holes and knotting securely on both sides. Join upper and lower legs. *Note:* When arms and legs are on the doll, lower pieces should overlap on the outside of the upper arm or leg.

Join legs and arms to body using ends of the twine that have been threaded through the body. Make an overhand knot to secure arms and legs to the body; trim excess twine.

ADDING THE HAT AND HAIR: Glue cotton or wool in place on the head and under the nose. (Refer to the photograph on page 122.)

From the ½-inch pine, cut a circle (hat brim) that measures 2½ inches in diameter. Center and glue the 2¼-inch length of 1½-inch-diameter dowel to the hat brim circle.

Paint the brim blue and the top of the hat ivory and red stripe. Using glue, fasten the hat to the doll's head.

Insert the dowel at the bottom of the doll's head into the body.

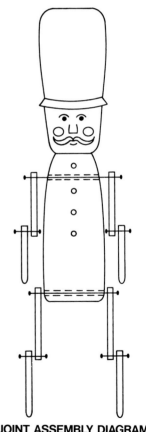

JOINT ASSEMBLY DIAGRAM

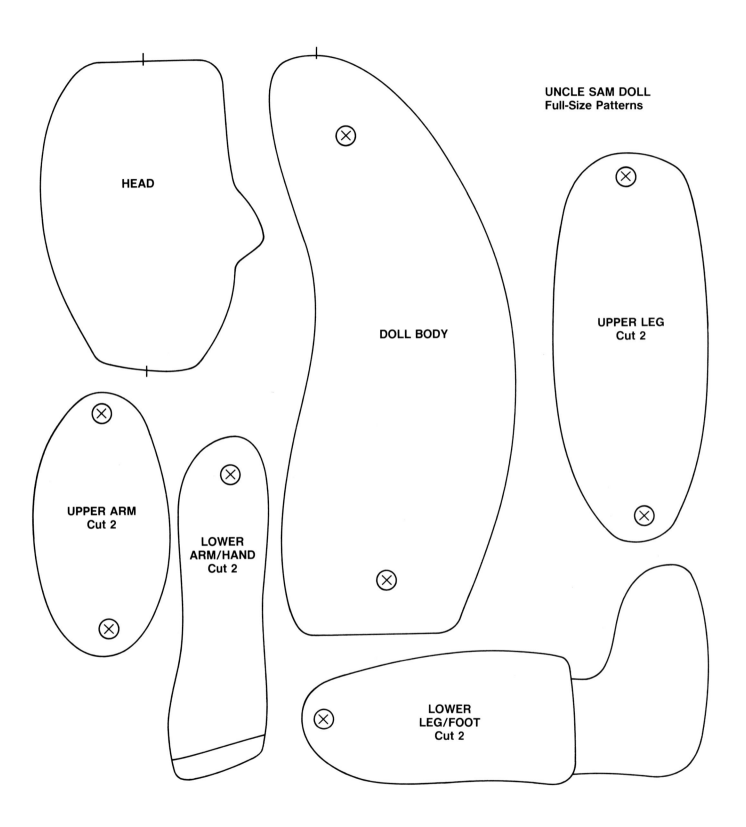

HEAD

DOLL BODY

UPPER LEG
Cut 2

UPPER ARM
Cut 2

LOWER
ARM/HAND
Cut 2

LOWER
LEG/FOOT
Cut 2

UNCLE SAM DOLL
Full-Size Patterns

Toy Soldier Knit Pullover

Shown on page 123.
Directions are given for children's Size 2-4. Changes for Sizes 4-6 and 6-8 follow in parentheses. Garment chest measurements = 23½ (25½, 27½) inches.

MATERIALS

Coats & Clark Red Heart Sport Yarn, Art. E. 281: 4 (5, 5) ounces of No. 1 white; 1 ounce *each* of No. 845 royal blue, No. 905 red, No. 722 light pink, No. 225 daffodil
Size 5 knitting needles
Large-eye yarn needle

Abbreviations: See page 187.
Gauge: Stockinette stitch on Size 5 needles: 6 sts = 1 inch; 8 rows = 1 inch.

INSTRUCTIONS

Note: Pullover is knit in white; wooden soldiers and sleeve design are added later in duplicate stitch.

BACK: With white, cast on 68 (74, 78) sts. Work in k 1, p 1 ribbing for 2 inches, inc 3 (3, 5) sts evenly spaced across last row—71 (77, 83) sts. Begin st st (k on right side, p on wrong side) and work until 12½ (13½, 14½) inches from beg, end with a p row.
Next row: K across, dec 1 st—70 (76, 82) sts. Work in k 1, p 1 ribbing for 1½ (2, 2) inches. Bind off loosely in ribbing.

FRONT: Work same as back.

SLEEVES: With white, cast on 40 (44, 46) sts. Work in k 1, p 1 ribbing for 1½ (2, 2) inches; inc 4 (6, 8) sts evenly spaced across last row—44 (50, 54) sts. Begin st st. Inc 1 st each edge every 6th row 8 (9, 10) times—60 (68, 74) sts. Work until 10½ (11½, 12) inches from beg. Bind off.

FRONT EMBROIDERY: There are two rows of wooden soldiers, with five soldiers in each row (see photograph on page 123). With contrasting color of sewing thread, sew a line of basting stitches up center of sweater front. Referring to Chart 1, *right,* align basting with center of soldier motif (marked by arrow); begin first soldier 1 inch up from ribbing. Following Chart 1 and the color key, work in duplicate stitch to complete first soldier. (For duplicate stitch diagram, see page 187.) Aligning soldier to basting, work second soldier 1 inch above the first. Sk 3 (4, 5) sts on each side of center soldiers; work another soldier to each side of the first two; repeat embroidery of soldiers until you have two rows with five soldiers in each row.

SLEEVE EMBROIDERY: Beg 4 (4¼, 4½) inches up from bottom of ribbing. Referring to Chart 2, *right,* work duplicate st with royal blue. Rep Chart 2 around both sleeves.

FINISHING: Dampen pieces; pin to measurements and allow to dry completely. With right sides facing, sew shoulder seams from shoulder edge for 2 inches on each side. Center and sew sleeves in place for 5 (5½, 6) inches below shoulder seam on each side. Sew underarm and side seams.

FRONT Chart 1

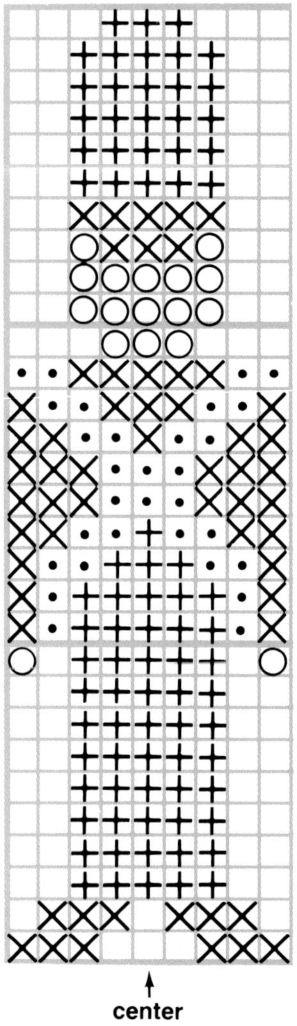

center

repeat

SLEEVE Chart 2

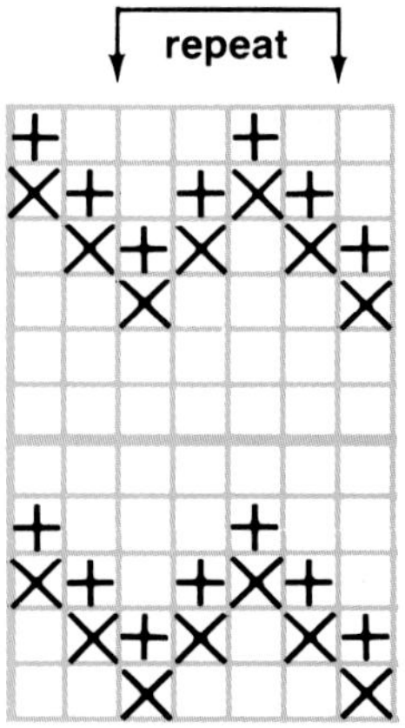

COLOR KEY

⊞ Royal Blue
⊠ Red
· Yellow
⊙ Light Pink

1 Square = 1 Stitch

Safety Tips for a Happy Holiday Season

As enchanting as Christmas is, your family's beautiful evergreen with its twinkling lights and glittering decorations can be a safety hazard. Take these precautions to guard against fire in your home during the holiday season.

CHOOSING A TREE: If you buy an artificial Christmas tree, make sure it's been tested for flammability by Underwriters Laboratories, Inc. and bears its seal of approval.

If you opt for a real tree, choose a fresh one. Fresh trees have a high moisture content; they are less likely to dry out and catch fire.

Test the needles by flexing them between your thumb and forefinger. The needles should bend but not break.

Store a fresh tree outdoors in a bucket of water, away from the sun and wind, until you're ready to bring it indoors and decorate it. Mist the tree occasionally to keep it moist.

SETTING UP A TREE: Just before you bring the tree inside, cut an inch or two off the bottom of the trunk so the tree can take in water easily.

Clean the tree stand with a small amount of household bleach mixed with water. The bleach kills microorganisms that reduce water intake.

Place the tree in a location away from the fireplace, radiator, and other heat sources. Avoid placing the tree where it interferes with the traffic pattern in your home, and see that it doesn't block a doorway.

Place a plastic drop cloth under the tree stand to protect the floor. All through the holiday season, keep the tree moist. Fill the tree stand with enough lukewarm water to cover the cut end of the trunk. Check the amount of water in the stand daily; a tree can consume as much as a gallon of water a day.

DECORATING A TREE: **Never use lighted candles on a tree or near evergreens or draperies.** Instead, use electric lights that have been checked for safety. (Look for the Underwriters Laboratories [UL] seal.)

Check each light set for broken or cracked sockets, frayed or bare wires, and loose connections. Repair or discard faulty light strings.

Replace burned-out bulbs on light strings. Never use aluminum foil or differently rated bulbs to replace burned-out bulbs. Keep light strings, decorative lamps, and other electrical decorations out of the reach of small children.

Fasten lights securely to the tree. If possible, avoid letting the bulbs touch the needles.

Don't put more than three sets of lights on a single extension cord. Use only one extension cord. Keep electrical cords away from the tree's water supply. Never use decorative strings of lights marked "For Indoor Use" on trees outdoors.

To prevent electrical shock, do not use electrical decorations on trees with metallic needles, leaves, or branches. Instead, use color spotlights above or beside a metallic tree.

Use decorations that are noncombustible or flame-resistant.

Use lead-free tinsel.

DISPOSING OF A TREE: If you've used a plastic drop cloth under the tree, after the holidays fold the drop cloth around the tree to catch needles and branches that may break off as you carry the tree outdoors.

Oversized plastic bags are available in the tree-trimming departments at many stores. The bags help make Christmas tree removal easy.

Burning evergreens in a fireplace is dangerous; flames can flare out and send sparks flying about the room. Give your tree to the garbage collector.

Equip your home with a UL-listed ABC-type fire extinguisher and smoke or heat detectors.

Always turn off the tree lights before leaving the house or going to bed.

WONDERFUL DESIGNS FROM TRADITIONAL COVERLETS

Brilliantly colored and richly patterned, the handwoven coverlets of America's past continue to provide a wealth of wonderful designs for today's crafter.

Inspired by the elaborate borders and motifs found on coverlets from colonial times, the knitted afghan, *left*, features bands of intricate detail. This cozy throw is worked in the round on circular needles. For authentic coloring, choose yarn in a rich shade of red and accent with tan.

For information on the sampler, *left*, turn the page.

Instructions for all projects in this section begin on page 134.

Designs borrowed from the handsome knitted afghan on pages 130 and 131 pattern the cross-stitch sampler, *opposite*. Worked entirely in rich red floss on a tan background of Aida cloth, this 15¼x17¾-inch wall hanging makes a striking accent for any room in your home.

The house, tree, and star elements are easily adapted to other materials. At *left*, these motifs are stitched on perforated paper, cut out, and glued to the face of a note card to create a holiday greeting. Or, stitch bunches more for tree trims and gift tags.

Knitted Coverlet-Style Afghan

Shown on pages 130 and 131.
Finished size is 54x64 inches.

MATERIALS
Aarlan Cristal (50-gram ball): 18
  balls of No. 4642 dark red; 9
  balls of No. 4635 tan
Size 8 circular knitting needle (36
  inches long)
Size H crochet hook
Tapestry needle; stitch markers

Abbreviations: See page 187.
Gauge: 5 sts = 1 inch.

INSTRUCTIONS
Note: This afghan is worked in the
round on circular needles. The three
purl stitches in each row are your
cutting seam allowance.

With red (main color), cast on 268
sts and join (place st marker), taking
care not to twist work. Purl 1 round.

Rnd 2: P 3 (cutting ridge); knit
around.

Rnd 3: Purl.

Rnds 4–5: Purl 3, knit around.

Note: Continue to work first 3 sts in
p throughout entire afghan and remaining 265 sts are knit.

Rnds 6–15: Referring to Chart 1,
opposite, work rows 1–10 from A–B
14 times, A–C once.

Rnds 16–56: Referring to Chart 2,
below, work rows 1–41 from A–C
once, B–C two times, ending with C–
D once. (*Note:* The shaded areas on
the chart are for placement only and
show work already completed. Do
not work this area.)

Rnds 57–66: Referring to Chart 3,
opposite, work rows 3–12 from A–B
14 times, A–C once.

Rnds 67–91: Work in MC (red).

**Rnds 92–101:* Referring to Chart
1 work rows 1–10 from A–B 14
times, A–C once.

Rnds 102–112: Referring to Chart
4, *opposite,* work rows 1–11 from A–
C once, B–C 10 times.

continued

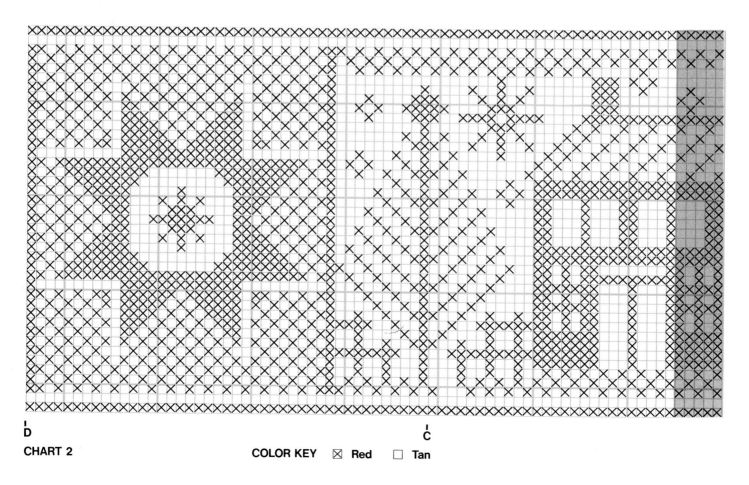

D   C

CHART 2   **COLOR KEY** ⊠ Red   ☐ Tan

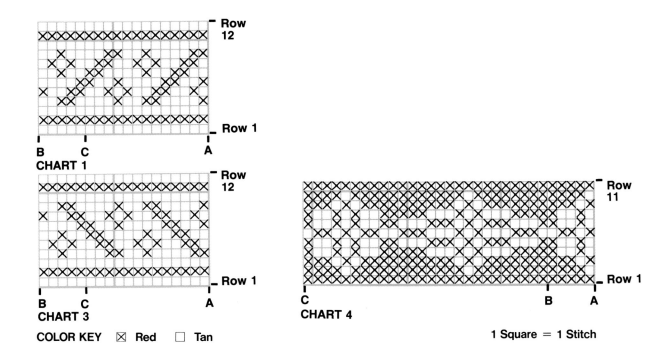

Row 12

Row 1

B **C** **A**

CHART 1

Row 12

Row 1

B **C** **A**

CHART 3

Row 11

Row 1

C **B** **A**

CHART 4

COLOR KEY ☒ Red ☐ Tan

1 Square = 1 Stitch

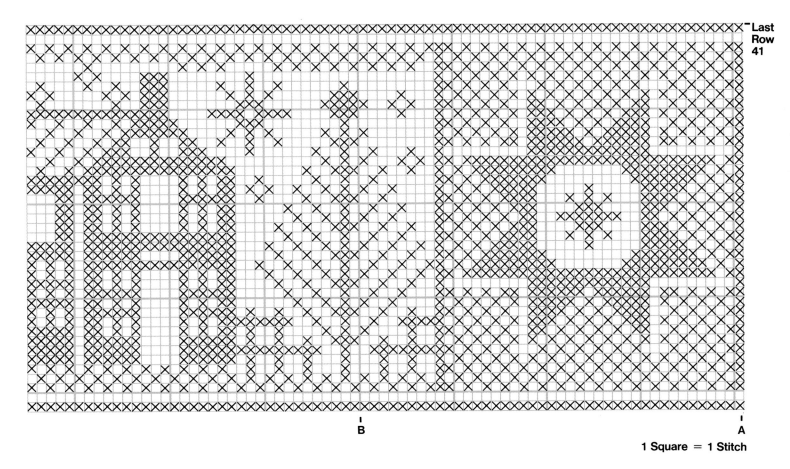

Last Row 41

B **A**

1 Square = 1 Stitch

135

Cross-Stitching Tips for Professional Results

Even though the cross-stitch technique is relatively straightforward, all good stitchers take a few basic steps to ensure the best results: They correctly position the stitchery on the fabric, they neatly begin and end threads, and they properly form stitches whether the stitches are adjacent or separated.

Here's how to make sure your work is as attractive and durable as that of an expert.

Preparing the fabric
Press out all creases and folds before stitching. Mist the fabric lightly with clean water and press with a warm iron. For stubborn folds, saturate the fabric or cover it with a wet press cloth before ironing.

All fabrics unravel along cut edges while being stitched. Raveled threads diminish the size of the background fabric and are bothersome when tangled with the embroidery threads. Bind the fabric edges with masking tape—simply fold the tape over the raw edges. An alternative to using masking tape is to machine-zigzag-stitch along the raw edges.

Working cross-stitches
To make a cross-stitch, pull a threaded needle from the wrong side of the fabric in a lower corner of the stitch. Carry the needle to the opposite upper corner of the stitch and insert it down through the fabric from front to back. This makes the first half of the cross-stitch.

To complete the stitch, make another stitch from an opposite corner that will cover the first half of the cross-stitch.

The first half may be worked from lower left to upper right *or* from lower right to upper left. (See diagram on page 186.) In any case, make sure all of the stitches are crossed *in the same direction*.

Beginning and ending threads
The best way to begin a cross-stitch is by using a waste knot. It is a temporary knot and will be clipped when no longer necessary. To begin, knot the end of your thread. Insert the needle into the *right* side of the fabric, about 4 inches from the placement of the first cross-stitch. Bring the needle up through the fabric and work the first cross-stitches. Stitch until the thread is used up or until the area using this color is complete.

To end a working thread, slip the needle under the previously stitched threads on the wrong side of the fabric for 1 to 1½ inches. Clip the thread.

Turn the piece to the right side and clip the beginning knot. Rethread the needle with the excess floss, push the needle through to the wrong side of the stitchery, and finish off the thread as directed above.

If you are working in areas that use a variety of thread colors, you may not wish to begin and end the thread for each element of the design. In these instances, carry the thread across the back of the fabric. To secure the thread, slip the threaded needle under the previously stitched crosses.

When carrying threads across the back of the fabric, tension is important. If your tension is too tight, the fabric tends to bunch up; if the tension is loose, the back of the stitching becomes messy, and threads tangle and twist or leave a shadow on the front of the work.

Correcting mistakes
Regardless of the complexity of a design, or of a stitcher's skill, mistakes are inevitable.

Small errors, such as working one or two additional stitches within a shaded area, or stitching the end of a leaf so it points in an opposite direction, will probably go unnoticed.

Some areas must be perfect. When border corners do not align, it's necessary to locate the error, remove the threads, and rework the stitches.

To remove stitches, use a pair of *sharp* scissors with tiny blades. Working from the back side, carefully snip away the threads and discard them. Use a pair of tweezers to pluck away stubborn threads.

Rnds 113–122: Following Chart 3 work rows 3–12 from A–B 14 times, A–C once.

Rnds 123–147: Work with MC (red).**

Rnds 148–312: Rep between **'s 3 times more.

Rnds 313–322: Referring to Chart 1 work rows 1–10 from A–B 14 times, A–C once.

Rnds 323–363: Work Chart 2 in reverse row order, from A–C once, B–C two times, ending with C–D once.

Rnds 364–373: Referring to Chart 1 work rows 3–12 from A–B 14 times, A–C once.

Rnds 374–376: With MC (red) K around.

Rnds 377–378: P around.

Bind off sts as to knit.

Block and spread open the (purl) cutting ridge.

With your sewing machine set on a straight stitch, sew two straight seams through first and last purl st of cutting ridge. Sew the entire length of the afghan. Cut the afghan open between the two rows of machine stitching.

BINDING: With No. 6 needle, cast on 8 sts and work in st st until binding measures the same length as cut edge of afghan. Repeat for a second binding. Using MC yarn, stitch bindings in place by hand. Sew pieces to the wrong side first then to the right side of afghan to cover machine stitching.

Lay the afghan out flat and block it gently. Weave in all loose ends on the wrong side.

FRINGE: Cut strands of yarn to measure 12 inches. Fold two strands in half, use crochet hook to pull through first stitch. Wrap ends around hook and pull ends through loop. Draw up tightly. Rep fringe across cast-on and bound-off ends, knotting fringe in every third stitch.

Paper Houses, Trees, And Stars

Shown on page 132.

MATERIALS
DMC embroidery floss as follows:
  1 skein *each* of No. 334 blue,
  No. 498 burgundy, and No. 986
  green
Ecru perforated paper
Tapestry needle

INSTRUCTIONS
The house, trees, and stars on the note cards on page 132 are elements extracted from the sampler pattern on pages 138–141.

Separate the floss into plies and use two plies to work the cross-stitches over one square of perforated paper. Stitch the houses in blue, the stars in red, and the trees in green. Do not pull floss too tightly as the paper will tear.

Using small, sharp scissors, cut out the shapes leaving one square beyond the stitching on all sides of the embroidery.

Glue shapes to note cards or attach a small piece of paper to the back side of each shape to make it freestanding.

Coverlet Pattern Cross-Stitch Sampler

Shown on pages 130–131, and 133. Finished size of sampler design is 15¼x17¾ inches.
Design is 137 stitches wide and 163 stitches high.

MATERIALS
22x25-inch piece of ecru 18-count
  Aida cloth
12 skeins of DMC No. 498
  burgundy embroidery floss
Embroidery hoop
Tapestry needle

INSTRUCTIONS
PREPARING THE PATTERN: Chart the complete sampler pattern on pages 138–141 onto graph paper using felt-tip marking pens. Or, you may work directly from our pattern. (*Note:* The shaded stitches indicate where the pattern overlaps. *Do not repeat these stitches.*)

TO STITCH THE DESIGN: Separate the embroidery floss and use three strands to work the cross-stitches over two threads of fabric.

Begin working at the upper left-hand corner. Leave 2 inches of plain fabric on all sides for mounting the finished needlework.

TO FINISH THE SAMPLER: Lightly press the stitchery on the back side of the fabric. Frame as desired.

COVERLET PATTERN CROSS-STITCH SAMPLER (Top Half)

COLOR KEY ☒ Red

1 Square = 1 Stitch

COVERLET PATTERN CROSS-STITCH SAMPLER (Bottom Half)

COLOR KEY ☒ Red

1 Square = 1 Stitch

141

ROMANTIC PASTELS FOR A SUN-DRENCHED PORCH

In warmer climates, where the December sun shines brightly and the winter air is warm, allow your holiday decorating spirit to run free with glorious pastel chintz fabrics.

Highly polished solid and floral fabrics are a pleasant surprise in the Christmas accessories, *above* and *right.*

Variations of the Hands-All-Around quilt pattern are highlighted in the stenciled floorcloth and repeated in the patchwork picture frame, tablecloth, and pillows.

Pieced, painted, or worked in cross-stitch, the star is just the right size for dressing the tree or topping off a special package. Turn the page for a closer look at the other projects.

Instructions begin on page 146.

Giving has long been one of the best parts of Christmas. The assortment of treasures in this chapter surely will delight your friends and loved ones.

The doll, *opposite,* begins with a simple stencil on muslin fabric. Machine-stitch the painted pieces together and dress her in holiday finery for a special child. Piece and embroider the stocking and fill it with small surprises for Christmas morning.

Embroider the handsome bird design, *right,* on cotton, and sew it into a pillow or pincushion. Or, stuff it with potpourri for an elegant drawer sachet.

The patchwork frame suggests yet another use of the Hands-All-Around quilt design. The open center can be used for a print, photo, or mirror.

Painted Wooden Star And Heart Ornaments

Shown on pages 142 and 143. Finished size is approximately 6 inches across at widest point.

MATERIALS

Scraps of ⅛-inch plywood
Acrylic paints in pink, red, blue, yellow, and green
Black permanent marker
Jigsaw
Drill
Clear fishing line

INSTRUCTIONS

Full-size patterns for the star and heart shapes are given *below*. Transfer the star and heart shapes to cardboard and cut out one template for each shape.

Trace around the shape on plywood. Using a jigsaw, cut out as many as you wish to paint.

Using cream-color acrylic paint, apply a base coat to each cutout.

The design on the heart ornament is the same as the design on the embroidered heart pillow on page 152, except that the ornament is smaller. Use the full-size pattern, *below right,* for the wooden hearts. (*Note:* On some of the ornaments, the design has been flopped for variety.)

Paint the bird and flower design with acrylic paints, referring to the embroidery pattern on page 152 for color suggestions.

Paint the star to resemble the triangle piecing of the soft-sculptured ornaments on pages 142 and 143. Use the black marker to draw "quilting" lines on each triangle.

Allow each color to dry thoroughly before applying the next color.

When all painting is completed, drill a hole in the top/center of the ornament. Insert ribbon or monofilament for hanging.

Cross-Stitch Star Ornament

Shown on pages 142 and 143. Finished size is 4 inches square.

MATERIALS

Two 5x5-inch scraps of 14-count Aida cloth in yellow or ecru
Embroidery floss in colors listed on color key
Polyester fiberfill

INSTRUCTIONS

Transfer design, *opposite,* onto graph paper, or work from our chart.

Separate the floss and use two strands over one thread of cloth. Follow the color key and the pattern to stitch one complete star for each ornament desired.

Trim the fabric to 4x4 inches. Cut a second piece of Aida for the backing. Topstitch the two squares together, wrong sides facing, ½ inch in on three sides. Stuff the ornament with fiberfill. Topstitch the fourth side closed. Pull the threads around the outside to create the fringe.

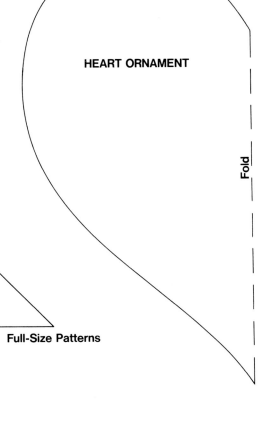

HEART ORNAMENT

Fold

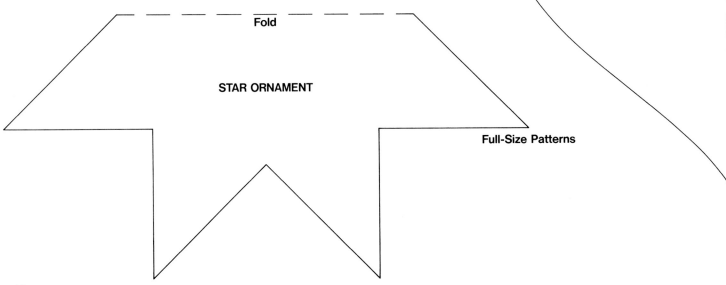

Fold

STAR ORNAMENT

Full-Size Patterns

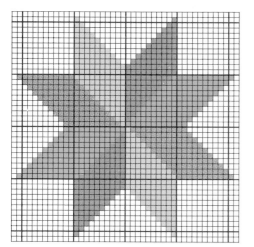

1 Square = 1 Stitch

COLOR KEY

	DMC	Bates
☐ Dk. Green	991	0189
☐ Lt. Green	993	0186
☐ Lt. Blue	794	0120
☐ Coral	3328	035

To make a hanger, cut a 10-inch length of each floss used. (Do not separate the strands.) Put all colors together. With a larger needle, run one end of all colors through the upper left-hand corner of the ornament. Knot the end. Run the second end through the upper right-hand corner. Knot the end.

Soft-Sculptured Star Ornaments

Shown on pages 142 and 143. Finished size is 5½ inches from point to point.

MATERIALS
Scraps of assorted fabrics in solid colors
Polyester fiberfill
Sewing thread
Covered buttons
Clear fishing line or ribbon (hanger)

INSTRUCTIONS
Transfer the full-size pattern for the F diamond on page 148 onto paper. Add ¼-inch seam allowances. Cut out eight diamonds in a variety of solid-color fabrics. Piece together eight diamonds for each ornament, referring to the photograph on page 142 for colors.

Cut a backing to match the pieced front. With right sides facing, stitch the back to the front. Leave an opening for turning. Turn right side out, stuff, and stitch opening closed.

Sew a covered button to the center front, tightening the thread to the back side to pull the star center inward. Use clear fishing line or ribbon for hanging.

Chintz Pillows

Shown on pages 142 and 143. Finished size of the Hands-All-Around pillow is 14 inches square without ruffles or piping; Star block pillow is 13½ inches square.

MATERIALS
Assorted scraps of solid and print cotton chintz fabrics
Polyester fiberfill
Contrasting fabric for piping or ruffle

INSTRUCTIONS
Transfer full-size pattern pieces A through E on page 148 onto tissue paper.

Note: Both pillows have been pieced using a combination of several of the full-size pattern pieces from the Hands-All-Around quilt block design. Refer to the diagrams on pages 149 and 150 for the arrangements shown. On the Hands-All-Around pillow shown on pages 142 and 143, D and E center shapes are cut as one piece from the floral chintz fabric.

The quilting design lends itself to hand-piecing because of the curved seams and the number of pieces that are "set in."

Piece each side of the Hands-All-Around design following the piecing diagram on page 149, *upper right.* Join them to the center (D/E) shape.

Note: The star pillow pattern is a combination of two of the half-star or "hands" sections.

TO FINISH THE PILLOWS: Cut a backing fabric to match the pieced front. Add piping or a ruffle from contrasting fabric. (*Note:* Complete directions for finishing pillows in a variety of ways appear on page 187.) With right sides facing, sew front to back on three sides. Turn pillow right side out. Stuff with polyester fiberfill. Stitch the fourth side closed.

Painted Floorcloth

Shown on pages 142 and 143. Finished size is 48½x68½ inches.

MATERIALS
52½x72½ inches heavy artist's canvas
PVA primer (polyurethane, varnish, acrylic)
Acrylic paint in the following colors: Green, medium pink, deep pink, blue, and yellow
Masking tape
Brushes
Stencil brushes
Stencil paper
Ruler
Crafts glue
Staple gun
Clear acrylic varnish

continued

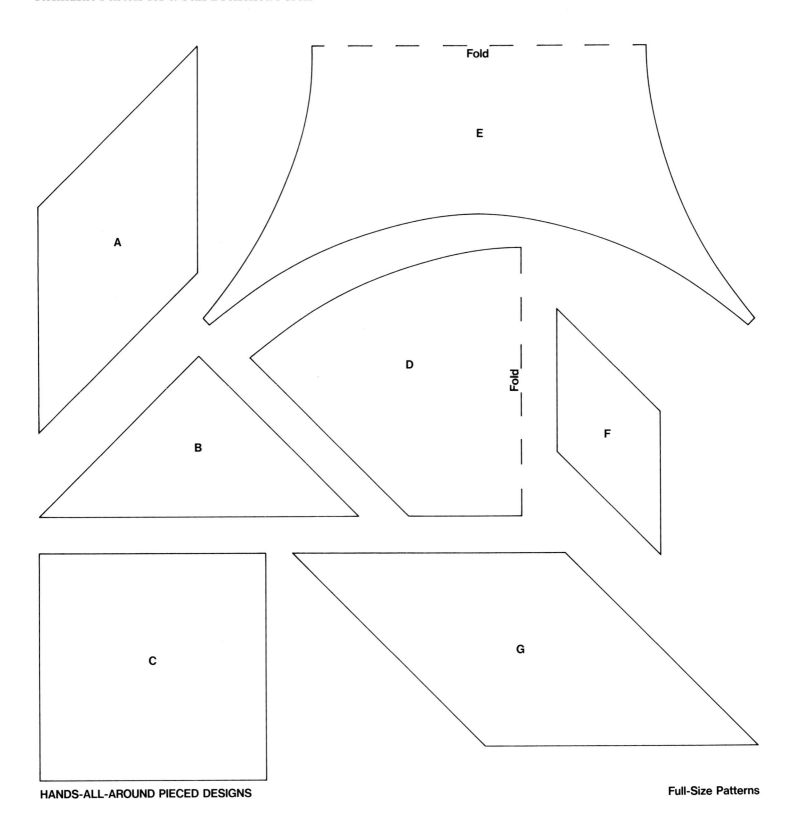

HANDS-ALL-AROUND PIECED DESIGNS

Full-Size Patterns

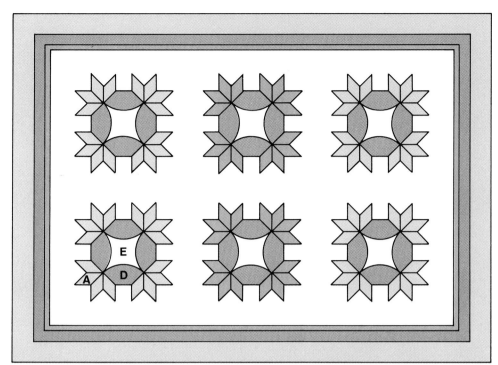

PAINTED FLOORCLOTH DIAGRAM

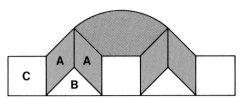

PIECING DIAGRAM (ONE BLOCK)

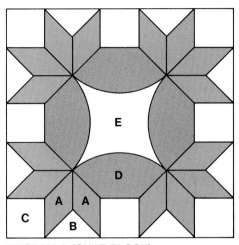

DIAGRAM A (QUILT BLOCK)

INSTRUCTIONS

Stretch and staple the artist's canvas to a "frame." (A piece of plywood works well.) Apply two coats of PVA primer (available in paint and hardware departments) to the front side of the canvas, allowing drying time between each coat. Lightly sand the canvas after the first coat is dry to ensure that the second coat will adhere properly.

Apply two coats of yellow paint for the background, allowing the first coat to dry thoroughly before going on to the second.

Use the full-size pattern pieces A, D, and E, *opposite,* and the placement diagram, *above,* to transfer the design to the canvas.

Paint the design on the canvas, allowing each color to dry before going on to the next color. Add the bands of color on the border last.

When all colors of paint are dry, cover the entire front of the cloth with a coat of clear varnish. Allow the cloth to dry thoroughly.

TO FINISH THE CLOTH: Remove the staples from the canvas and frame. Measure 2 inches beyond the completed edge of the design; cut along this line. Turn the canvas over to the unfinished side. Measure two inches inward along all four sides; draw a pencil line. Cut the canvas from the corner in to the drawn line. Turn the edges inward and trim to form a smooth, mitered corner.

Fold all raw edges inward to the 2-inch line. Glue. Weight the "hem" with something heavy (boards, bricks, books) to hold it flat until it has adequate time to dry. When dry (12 hours), turn the rug upright. Apply a second coat of varnish to finish the rug. (*Note:* If the rug will be used in an unusually high-traffic area, you may choose to put a third coat of varnish on the top of the rug.)

Hands-All-Around Square Tablecloth

Shown on pages 142 and 143. Finished size is 31 inches square, excluding the ruffle.

MATERIALS

2 yards of 54-inch-wide solid-color chintz fabric for the backing, borders, and block centers
¼ yard of solid-color chintz for the "hands" corners
¼ yard of solid-color chintz for the squares and triangles around the "hands"
Scraps of floral chintz for centers
1½ yards print for ruffle
Batting

continued

INSTRUCTIONS

Full-size pattern pieces A through E are used in this project. Refer to the photograph on pages 142 and 143 for fabric suggestions. Piece the Hands-All-Around block following the diagrams on page 149. Each block will be 14 inches square, including ¼-inch seam allowances.

Join the blocks using 2-inch solid chintz borders. Make the 3-inch-wide ruffle and baste to the table-cloth top. (Tips for ruffles and piping appear on page 187.)

Cut a backing and batting to measure 31½ inches square. Lay backing on the top, right sides facing; lay batting on top of backing. Machine-stitch around all sides, leaving a 6-inch opening for turning. Turn; stitch the opening closed.

Star Table Runner

Shown on page 145.
Finished size is 51¼x11¾ inches.

MATERIALS

1 yard of 54-inch-wide medium-rose chintz fabric
Scraps of solid blue, green, and dark-rose chintz fabric
Scraps of yellow print chintz fabric
Quilt batting
Piping

INSTRUCTIONS

Full-size pattern pieces A, B, and C on page 148 are used for the runner.

Piece each star block by joining eight A diamonds. (*Note:* The star is the same as the center of the block in Diagram B, *above.*) Stitch C squares into each corner and B triangles between star points on top, bottom, and each side. Each block in the runner is 8¾ inches square (includes ¼-inch seams).

Cut six 2¼x8¾-inch strips of solid medium-rose chintz fabric. Join the

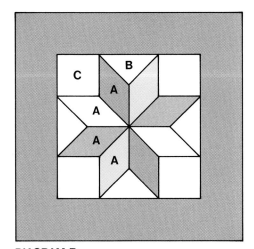

DIAGRAM B

star blocks using these strips. Sew an additional strip to each end of the joined star blocks.

Cut two 2¼x51¾-inch strips of solid medium-rose chintz fabric. Right sides facing, sew strips along sides of table runner top.

Baste contrasting piping to the outside edges of the table runner top. Cut a backing and batting to measure 51¾x12¼ inches. Lay the backing on top with right sides facing; lay batting on top of the backing. Machine-stitch around three edges. Turn; stitch opening closed.

Picture Frame

Shown on pages 142 and 145.
Finished size is 14x14 inches.

MATERIALS

Assorted scraps of solid and print cotton chintz fabrics
14-inch square of solid-color chintz fabric
14-inch square of quilt batting
14-inch square of foam-core board
3½ yards of piping
Masking tape
Two plastic curtain rings

INSTRUCTIONS

Transfer full-size A, B, and C pattern pieces on page 148 onto paper.

Note: The design for the frame is the same design as the pillow Diagram A on page 149 except that the center motif (combination of D and E pieces) has been omitted. Piece the design following the directions for the pillow top on page 147.

Machine-baste along the eight-sided edge at the inside of the pattern; stitch piping to this edge.

Stitch piping around the outside edges of the 14-inch pieced square.

Cut a 14-inch square from foam-core board. Trace the opening for the mirror onto the foam-core square. Cut out the center using pattern pieces D and E to determine how much and what shape to cut. Cut a piece of quilt batting to fit between the pieced top and the foam-core.

Position the pieced frame front atop the batting and the foam-core, and tape the raw edges of the fabric to the back side. Tape the picture (or a mirror) to the back of the frame. Cut a 14½-inch square of solid-color fabric; press the edges under ¼ inch.

Hand-stitch backing in place.

Patchwork Chintz Christmas Stocking

Shown on page 144.
Finished size of stocking is 9½ inches wide x 14½ inches deep.

MATERIALS

½ yard of solid chintz fabric for front, back, cuff, and piping
Scraps of solid chintz in pink, rose, and blue-green
Scraps of floral chintz
¼ yard of cotton for lining
¼ yard of polyester fleece
1½ yards of purchased cording
Embroidery floss in lavender, pink, and green

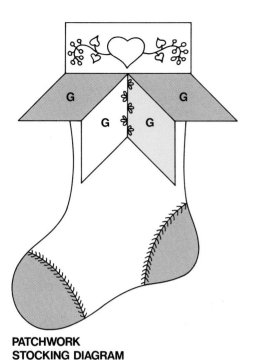

**PATCHWORK
STOCKING DIAGRAM**

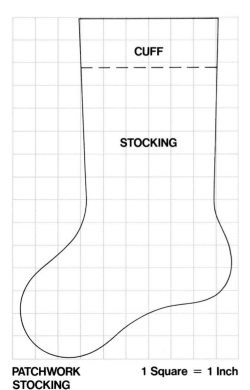

**PATCHWORK
STOCKING**   1 Square = 1 Inch

INSTRUCTIONS

Enlarge the stocking pattern, *below left*, on paper. (Add ¼-inch seam allowances to all pieces before cutting fabric.) From solid chintz, cut one stocking front and one back. Do not cut along the dashed line. From floral chintz, cut toe and heel patches using the diagram, *left,* as a guide.

Back stocking front and back with fleece. Baste floral toe and heel pieces in place, tucking under raw edges of patches atop stocking body. Use three strands of embroidery floss and the featherstitch on the inside edge of the floral chintz. (See the photograph on page 144.)

Baste cording around the sides and bottom of the stocking front.

Sew the back to the front, leaving the top open. Cut two stocking shapes from cotton. Sew two pieces in the same manner, leaving an opening along the stocking bottom.

TO MAKE THE CUFF: Cut a strip of fabric 3x13 inches. Locate the center of the cuff strip.

Center and transfer the heart and vine design on page 152 to the strip of fabric. Using three strands of floss, embroider leaves, vine, and berries. Use the straight stitch on the stems, and the satin stitch to fill in leaves and berries. (Stitch diagrams appear on page 186.)

Machine-appliqué a rose fabric heart in the center. Carefully press the embroidery on the back side. Cut a matching backing for the cuff. Back the cuff strip with fleece. With right sides facing, sew the cuff to the cuff backing along the top edge; turn right side out.

Sew the cuff to the stocking, placing the lining side of the cuff together with the right side of the stocking. Join the ends of the cuff at the back center of the stocking.

Insert the stocking into the stocking lining, right sides facing. Sew around the top of the stocking. Turn stocking right side out through the hole in the lining; stitch lining closed. Tuck lining into the stocking.

TO MAKE THE PIECED TRIANGLE EDGE: Cut eight G diamonds from assorted solid chintz fabric, using the pattern on page 148. Add ¼-inch seam allowances before cutting.

Piece two sets of four diamonds together, alternating colors. With right sides facing, sew the two sets together, leaving the long straight edge open for turning. Turn right side out; press flat. Use a variety of embroidery stitches along the seam lines to give the edging a crazy-quilt look. Tuck the pieced-triangle trim under the embroidered cuff; tack the cuff down in place over the triangles. (Refer to the photograph on page 144 for guidance.)

Heart Pillow

Shown on pages 142 and 145.
Finished size is 6x7 inches,
excluding ruffle.

MATERIALS

Two 9-inch squares of muslin (or any closely woven ecru or white fabric)
¼ yard of fabric for ruffle (optional)
Embroidery floss in lavender, gold, medium green, dark green, and tangerine
Polyester fiberfill
Cording
Tracing paper
Light-color dressmaker's carbon

INSTRUCTIONS

From ecru or white fabric, cut two 9-inch squares. Trace the full-size pattern on page 152 onto tracing paper. Center the design and use dressmaker's carbon to transfer the design onto the pillow-front fabric square.
continued

151

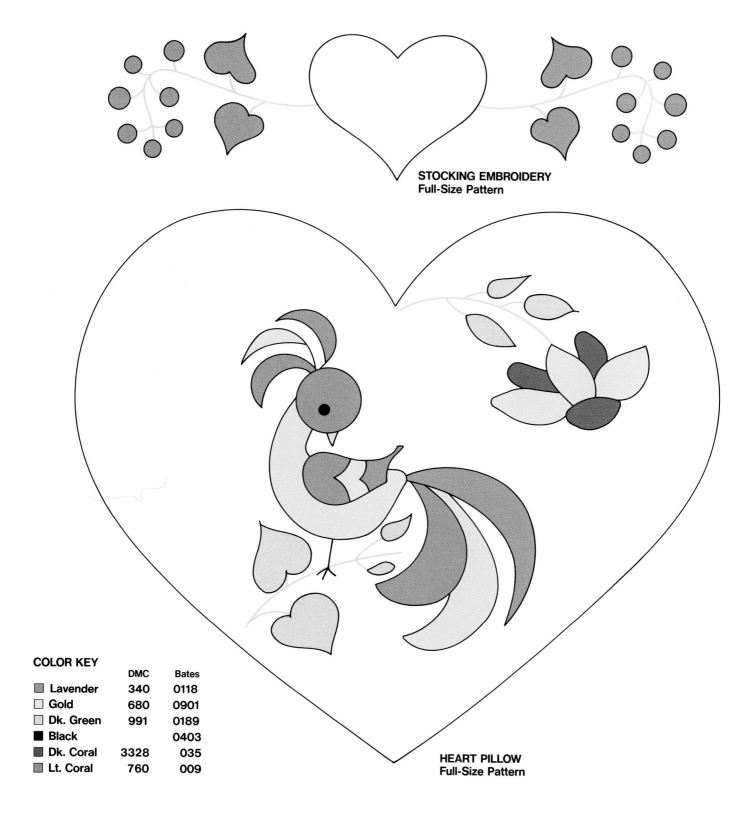

STOCKING EMBROIDERY
Full-Size Pattern

COLOR KEY

		DMC	Bates
	Lavender	340	0118
	Gold	680	0901
	Dk. Green	991	0189
	Black		0403
	Dk. Coral	3328	035
	Lt. Coral	760	009

HEART PILLOW
Full-Size Pattern

Use three strands of floss for all embroidery. Refer to the pattern on page 152 for color suggestions. Use outline stitch for branches and satin stitch to fill in spaces. (Stitch diagrams are on page 186.)

Lightly press the finished embroidery on the back side. Cut out the front and backing. Finish following general instructions on page 187.

Stenciled Doll

Shown on pages 143 and 144. Finished size is 21 inches tall.

MATERIALS
⅞ yard of 45-inch-wide muslin fabric (body, panty, slip, dress)
⅜ yard of 45-inch-wide rose fabric (dress)
1⅓ yards of ⅛-inch-wide elastic
1 yard of ⅞-inch-wide rose satin ribbon (hair bow)
2 yards of ¼-inch-wide rose satin ribbon (shoe bows)
Polyester fiberfill (stuffing)
Black and brown embroidery floss
Two small snaps
Rose, dark rose, green, light brown, dark brown, and white stencil paints
Stencil plastic
Stencil knife
Stencil paintbrush
Tracing paper
Permanent marking pen
Clear adhesive-backed plastic

INSTRUCTIONS
Note: All patterns and measurements include ¼-inch seam allowances unless otherwise stated. Sew all seams with right sides facing.

Patterns on pages 154 and 155 are full size. Because of space allowance, you must join lower head line AB to body piece at AB. This represents one pattern piece when joined. Extend the leg piece at the broken line so that the total leg/foot pattern piece is 11¾ inches long.

Transfer the head/body pieces and the legs to muslin. Do not cut out shapes until stenciling is finished.

In addition to the pattern pieces, cut one 24x6-inch muslin rectangle for the panty, and one 40x9-inch muslin rectangle for the slip. Cut two 14x4½-inch rectangles from rose for the sleeves, one 45x6-inch rose skirt top, and one 45x3-inch rose skirt bottom. Cut one 12x1-inch rose neck binding on the bias of the fabric. From muslin, cut one 45x2½-inch skirt inset band.

TO STENCIL THE DESIGN: Place stencil plastic atop paper patterns and, using permanent marking pen, trace hair front and back, eyes, eyelids, nose, mouth, and shoe front and back. Cut out each pattern; cut a ¾-inch-diameter circle stencil pattern for the cheeks. For the interior lines of hair and shoe front, place adhesive-backed plastic atop paper patterns. Trace with a pencil and cut out. Peel away the backing and press into position directly onto the fabric.

Stencil the hair and shoes light brown, the eyes and eyelids dark brown, and the nose and lips dark rose. Stencil the cheeks. Straight-stitch the eyelashes with two strands of brown floss. Accent the eye with a dot of white paint.

For the dress, center the floral motif on the bodice front and stencil the flower rose and the leaves green. Center and repeat motif for entire muslin skirt band.

Remove the adhesive-backed plastic and cut out fabric body pieces.

For the doll
BODY AND LEGS: Sew the legs together in pairs, matching fronts to backs and leaving the tops open. Clip the curves and turn to the right side. Stuff, then sew across the tops.

Sew together body front and back, leaving the bottom open. Restitch the neck and underarm. Clip the curves and turn to the right side. Sew together legs and body front, matching the raw edges.

Stuff the arms and stitch across the joint using the dashed lines on the pattern as a guide. Stuff the head and body. Turn under raw edge of body back and stitch closed.

For the clothes
PANTY: Press under and stitch both long edges for casings. Cut one piece of elastic to fit waist and a second piece long enough to fit around both legs. (Add 1 inch to each piece.) Pull elastic through each casing with a small safety pin. Sew together short edges. Sew a short inner leg seam at the center of the bottom casing.

SLIP: Narrow-hem one long edge. Press under other long edge for casing and stitch. Cut elastic to fit waist; pull through casing with a small safety pin. Sew together short edges.

DRESS: Sew together front and back bodice shoulder seams. Narrow hem the center back edges. Encase neck with bias binding.

Sew gathering stitches across one long edge of the sleeves. For casings, press under other long edge and stitch. Cut elastic to fit arm and pull through casing with a safety pin. Pin sleeve into armhole, pull center gathers to fit, and stitch. Sew together sleeve and bodice side seams.

Sew together long edges of skirt top, stenciled band, and the skirt bottom. Turn skirt fabric under 1½ inches for hem and sew. Sew gathering stitches across top, pull to fit bodice, and stitch together. Sew together lower skirt back, using a ½-inch seam. Sew snaps to neck and waist of bodice back opening.

BOWS: Attach wide rose ribbon hair bow and small ribbon shoe bows.

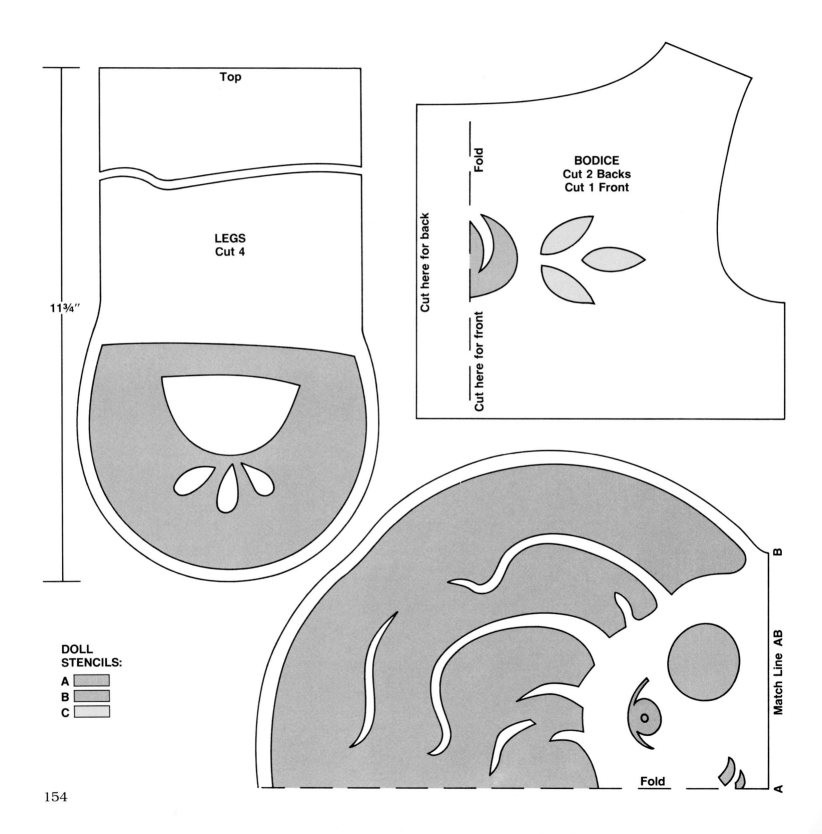

Top

LEGS
Cut 4

11¾"

BODICE
Cut 2 Backs
Cut 1 Front

Fold

Cut here for back

Cut here for front

DOLL
STENCILS:

A
B
C

B

Match Line AB

Fold

A

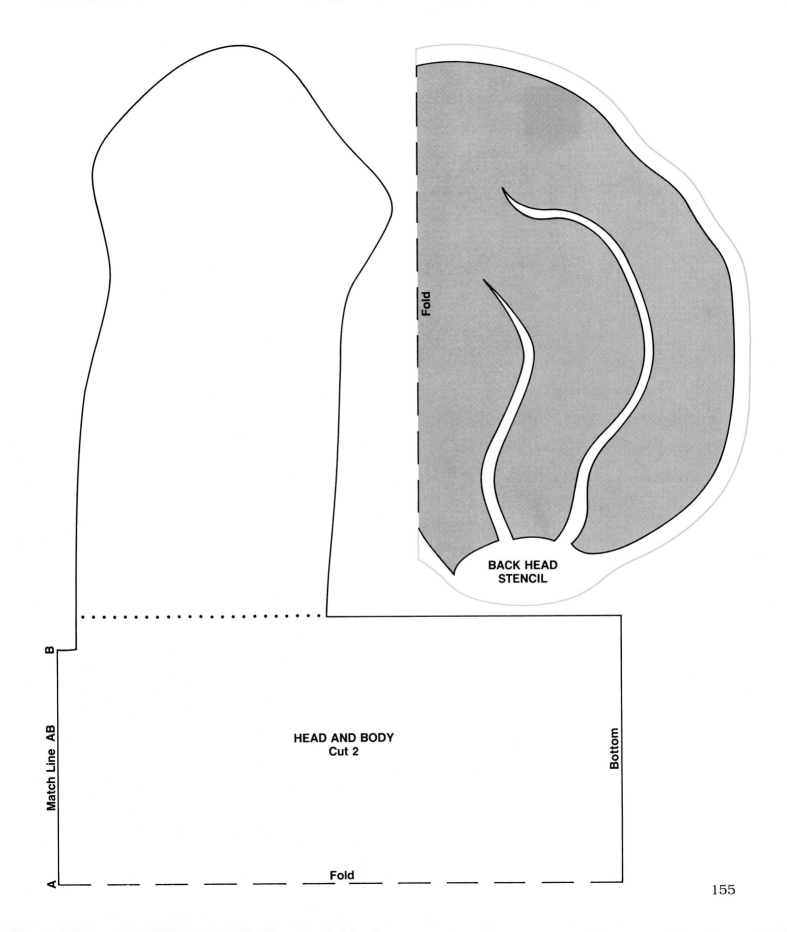

Fold

BACK HEAD
STENCIL

B

Match Line AB

HEAD AND BODY
Cut 2

Bottom

A

Fold

155

A COUNTRY CHRISTMAS IN THE CITY

Capture the spirit of an old-fashioned Christmas with garlands of greenery and traditional holiday colors. Handmade decorations enhance the country spirit of this sleek city condo.

Pine boughs wrapped in red ribbon accent the hand-painted ornaments, *above* and *right.* Clear glass Christmas balls and acrylic paints are all you need to make these elegant tree trims.

A painted evergreen and holly design is also used to dress up the pre-cut picture mats, *right.*

Cross-stitched bells and a handsome wool plaid fabric combine here to create an heirloom-quality tablecloth and photo album. The larger bells on the tablecloth are stitched on 12-count waste canvas basted to broadcloth.

Instructions and patterns for all projects follow on page 160.

A COUNTRY CHRISTMAS IN THE CITY

Dressed in her holiday best, the Victorian doll, *below,* is certain to delight doll lovers of all ages. Her body is crafted from muslin and her clothing is fashioned from taffeta trimmed with scraps of elegant lace.

Embroidered facial features and twisted yarn curls complete this enchanting doll that measures a full 25 inches tall.

A distinctive border of patchwork quilt patterns sets the stage for the heartfelt sentiment of the sampler, *opposite.*

Preserve precious photographs of Christmases past in an album designed for precisely that purpose. The album cover, *above,* features a band of holiday bells worked in counted cross-stitch that is centered on a red and green plaid wool fabric.

Painted Picture Mattings

Shown on pages 156–157, and 159. Finished size of mats shown is 8x10 inches (small) and 11x14 inches (large).

MATERIALS

Precut picture mats or mat board for cutting your own
Acrylic paint in light green, medium green, dark green, and red
Artist's brushes

INSTRUCTIONS

Note: The full-size patterns, *right,* can be adjusted to fit almost any mat size or shape. Purchase precut mats or make your own. The prints in the photograph on pages 156, 157, and 159 have been double-matted, with the painting on the top mat.

Trace patterns onto tissue; transfer the designs to the precut mats. Paint the designs with acrylics, referring to pattern for colors. Paint the ribbon first, the leaves and berries next, and the evergreen boughs last. Use a very fine liner or script brush for the evergreens, applying different shades of green to each bough.

Allow each color to dry thoroughly. Frame as desired.

Painted Christmas Balls

Shown on pages 156 and 157.

MATERIALS

Purchased clear glass Christmas balls
Denatured alcohol
Dressmaker's carbon
Acrylic paint in cream, light green, medium green, dark green, red, and gold
Acrylic matte-finish varnish
Artist's brushes

INSTRUCTIONS

Rub the clear glass balls with denatured alcohol to cut the gloss finish.

Paint all sides of the balls with cream-colored acrylic paint.

Transfer the pattern, *below,* onto tissue. Using dressmaker's carbon, transfer the designs to the balls.

Paint the designs with acrylics, referring to the pattern for colors. Paint the ribbon first, the fruit second, and the evergreen boughs last. Use a very fine liner or script brush for the evergreen, applying different shades of green to each bough.

Allow each color to dry before going to the next color. Spray with the acrylic varnish to protect design.

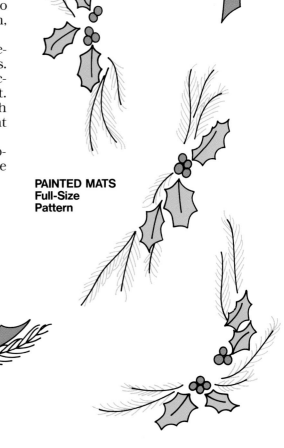

**PAINTED MATS
Full-Size
Pattern**

**CHRISTMAS BALL
Full-Size Pattern**

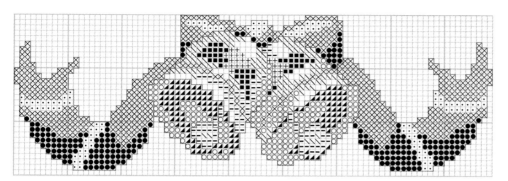

CROSS-STITCHED PHOTO ALBUM COVER COLOR KEY

1 Square = 1 Stitch

		DMC	Bates				DMC	Bates
□	White		0402		◉	Dark Red	815	044
◪	Green	986	0245		◪	Brown	434	310
⊞	Bright Red	666	046		◯	Dark Gold	782	0308
·	Light Red	892	028		⊟	Light Gold	783	0306
⊠	Medium Red	347	019		◺	Yellow	743	0297

Cross-Stitched Photo Album Cover

Shown on pages 156–157, and 159. Finished size of album shown is 8x14 inches.

MATERIALS

4½x16-inches of 12-count Aida cloth
Embroidery floss in colors listed on the color key
Purchased photograph album
¼ yard of plaid fabric (½ yard of wool if the album is large)
½ yard of cotton for lining
Gold cording
Quilt batting
Embroidery hoop
Tapestry needle

INSTRUCTIONS

PREPARING THE PATTERN: Chart the complete pattern, *above*, onto graph paper using felt-tip marking pens. Or, you may work directly from our pattern.

TO STITCH THE DESIGN: Separate the embroidery floss and use three strands of floss to stitch over one thread of Aida fabric.

Locate center of pattern and center of fabric. Begin working there. After stitching is complete, leave at least 1 inch of fabric on the top and bottom of the design, and 4 inches on each end of the design for mounting into the album cover. Press the back side of the finished piece of cross-stitch before assembling the cover.

ASSEMBLY: Measure the height and width of the cover when the book is open flat. Add ½ inch all around for seam allowances. From plaid fabric, cut an album cover to fit this measurement; cut batting and cotton lining to match. Curve the edges of the fabric, batting, and lining if the edges of the album are curved.

Turn under the top and bottom edges of the cross-stitched Aida fabric. Press flat. Hand-stitch in place on the album cover top, referring to the photograph on page 159. Stitch cording into place at the same time.

Cut flaps that will fit over the inside edges of the front and back covers. Measure top-to-bottom length of

the album. Make flap that length, plus ½ inch all around, and approximately 6 inches wide. (Cut two pieces from plaid wool fabric.)

If you are using cording, as shown in the photographs, measure around the entire outside edge of the cover when the album is lying flat and open. Cut a piece of cording to that length, plus one inch.

Lay the batting on a flat surface; top with album cover plaid fabric piece, right side up. Hand-baste the gold cording around the cover. Lay the plaid flap fabric pieces in place at each end with right sides of the fabric front and flap facing. Machine-stitch through all layers. Clip curves.

Hand-stitch the lining in place on the back side of the batting, turning top and bottom of fabric inward to conceal raw edges. Turn album cover right side out and fit over album.

Cross-Stitched Bells Tablecloth

Shown on pages 156 and 157. Finished size is 58 inches in diameter, excluding ruffle.

MATERIALS

1⅔ yards of 60-inch-wide white broadcloth (a high-quality white sheet will work)
1 yard plaid wool fabric
Embroidery floss in colors listed on the color key
One 7x16-inch piece of 12-count waste canvas for each bell motif
Embroidery hoop
Tapestry needle
Gold cording

INSTRUCTIONS

PREPARING THE PATTERN: Chart pattern, *above*, onto graph paper using felt-tip marking pens. Or, work directly from our pattern.

continued

TO STITCH THE DESIGN: Cut white fabric to form a 60-inch-diameter circle. Baste five strips of waste canvas evenly spaced around tablecloth edge. Refer to photograph on pages 156 and 157 for design placement.

Separate the embroidery floss and use three strands of floss to work the cross-stitches over two squares of waste canvas. This will give you six cross-stitches per inch.

After the design is stitched, trim waste canvas to within ¼ inch beyond stitching. Dampen stitchery with warm water; gently pull out threads of waste canvas from beneath cross-stitches.

When fabric is dry, press the back side with a dry iron.

TO FINISH THE TABLECLOTH: Cut plaid fabric into 6-inch-wide strips. Piece short ends of strips together to make a band that measures 360 inches long; then sew two ends together so that you have one large circle of fabric. Hem one long edge of the plaid fabric, turning under ¼ inch twice.

Run a gathering thread along the other edge of the long strip; pull to gather. With right sides facing, baste cording and then the gathered ruffle to outside edge of white tablecloth. Lightly press finished tablecloth.

Country Christmas Sampler

Shown on page 158.
Finished design area measures 14x16½ inches.

MATERIALS

22x24½-inch piece of 14-count
   Aida cloth
Embroidery floss as follows: 4
   skeins of red and 5 skeins of
   green

continued

162

A COUNTRY CHRISTMAS WARMS THE HEART

1 Square = 1 Stitch

COLOR KEY   ■ Green   ⊠ Red

163

INSTRUCTIONS

PREPARING THE PATTERN: Chart the complete pattern on pages 162 and 163 onto graph paper using felt-tip marking pens. Or, you may work directly from our pattern. (The shaded stitches on the portion of the pattern on page 163 indicate where the pattern on page 162 overlaps. *Do not repeat these stitches*.)

TO STITCH THE DESIGN: Separate the floss and use two strands of floss to work the cross-stitches over one thread of Aida fabric.

Locate the center of the pattern and the center of the fabric. Begin working there. Leave 4 inches of plain fabric on all sides for mounting the finished needlework.

TO FINISH THE SAMPLER: Lightly press the stitchery on the back side of the fabric. Frame as desired.

Victorian Doll

Shown on page 159.
Finished size is 25 inches tall.

MATERIALS
For the doll
⅝ yard of muslin
Polyester fiberfill
Dressmaker's carbon
Graph paper
1 skein of 4-ply brown yarn
Hair spray
Plastic wrap
Brown thread
½-inch-diameter dowel
Scraps of black, brown, and pink embroidery floss
Embroidery needle and hoop
Powdered rouge
Eye shadow
Dental floss

For the clothes
1 yard of burgundy taffeta
⅓ yard each of muslin and white voile
2 yards of narrow lace trim
4-inch-deep triangular scrap of lace
24 inches of narrow elastic
⅓ yard of narrow black ribbon
5 small snaps
Scraps of gray vinyl and black felt
10 black beads

INSTRUCTIONS

The full-size pattern pieces for the doll appear on pages 166–168. *Note:* The leg patterns must be joined at the AB line to make the complete leg pattern. The doll body patterns must be joined at the CD lines to make the complete body pattern. Trace the patterns onto paper; transfer the shapes to muslin.

Patterns include ¼-inch seam allowances. Sew pattern pieces together with right sides facing, unless otherwise noted.

Doll

FACE: Trace the face pattern onto one head shape and, referring to the stitch diagrams on page 186, embroider the features before cutting out the pieces as follows: With a single strand of black floss, use satin stitches to fill in the eyebrows. Outline eyelids and nose. Use black straight stitches for lashes. With three strands of floss, satin-stitch brown irises and pink lips. Add a black French knot for the pupil of each eye. Highlight eyelids and cheeks using powdered eye shadow and rouge.

BODY/HEAD: Cut all pattern pieces from muslin. Sew body darts, then stitch body pieces together, leaving neck edge open. Clip curves, turn, and stuff.

Sew head darts; trim to ¼ inch. Stitch head pieces together, leaving neck open. Clip curves, turn, and stuff firmly. Sew head to body using dental floss; add stuffing if needed.

ARMS: Sew arms together in pairs, leaving openings for turning. Clip curves, turn, and stuff. Sew openings closed. Stitch to shoulders.

LEGS: Stitch legs together in pairs, leaving opening at tops. Clip curves, turn, and stuff to within 1½ inches of tops. Turn raw edges at tops inward and sew closed. Sew legs to bottom of body.

HAIR: Hair is constructed in two sections using one skein of 4-ply brown yarn. For front section, wrap yarn 40 times around a 10½-inch length of cardboard . Cut a 1x7½-inch strip of muslin. Slip the yarn off the cardboard and stitch one end of the yarn loops down the center of the muslin strip lengthwise (do not cut loops.)

Fold strip in half lengthwise and center on doll's forehead with raw edges facing toward crown. Position the strip ½ inch down from center front dart and curve strip around the front of the face. Hand-stitch the strip in place, tucking in raw edges on the short end.

For the second hair section, cut 90 strands of yarn, each 48 inches long. Center the strands across a 1x5-inch strip of muslin. Machine-stitch yarn to the strip, forming a center part.

Position the muslin strip across the center top of the head, running from front to back, with the part beginning at the edge of the front hair section. Stitch the strip in place. Smooth the yarn strands evenly over the crown and hand-stitch the yarn around the head approximately 4 inches down from the center part.

STYLING THE BACK HAIR: To make curls, begin with the back section of yarn. Start at the center back and work toward the front, curling one section at a time. Divide each side into four equal groups of yarn. Thread a needle with a double strand of brown thread, knot the end, and set it aside. Starting at the center back, spray one group of strands with a light coat of hair spray (protect the doll with plastic wrap).

Starting at the bottom of the strands, wrap yarn around the ½-inch dowel. Roll it toward the center back to make one long vertical curl.

Slip the curl off the dowel. Slide the threaded needle through the curl and draw the needle through the knot at the end to hold the loops of the curl together. Stitch the top of the curl to the doll's head, and stitch again at intervals down the length of the curl to the base of the neck. Make two curls for this side and attach as before. Repeat for the other side of the head. There should now be six vertical sausage curls along the back of the head.

Grasp the last group of yarn strands on either side and pull gently to center back. Make two small sausage curls to hang over the top of six larger curls; tack curls in place.

STYLING THE FRONT HAIR: Pull the yarn up and back away from the face on one side. Twist all strands together into a soft roll around the front of the doll's face. Tack the strands to the head about ear level. Now divide the looped ends into five or six groups. Slide the loops of one group over the end of a pencil; turn the pencil in a circle to tightly twist the strands together. Slip the pencil out, holding on to the twisted end of the loops. Fold the twist in half, allowing two halves to twist around each other. Tack the ends to the head. Repeat for each group of yarn on one side, then repeat for the other side. Arrange yarn curls gracefully around sides and front of the face.

For the clothing
Enlarge the clothing patterns on pages 168 and 169 onto paper; trace the pieces onto fabrics.

Note: Add ¼-inch seam allowances to all pieces. Sew pattern pieces together with right sides facing, unless otherwise noted.

BLOOMERS: Cut two legs from voile. Hem the bottom edges and topstitch the narrow lace trim along the bottom of each leg. Stitch two tucks in each bloomer leg. Stitch leg seams; sew the right leg to the left leg. Turn under the top edge and sew to make the casing for the elastic, leaving an opening. Insert the elastic, fitting it to the doll's waist, and tie it off.

SLIP: Cut a 9¼x22½-inch rectangle from voile. Sew the short ends for center back seam. Turn up one edge to right side of slip to make the hem and topstitch lace trim to cover the raw edges. Make casing for the elastic at the waist edge; insert elastic, pull up to fit waist, and secure.

BODICE: Cut front and backs from the taffeta. Make four tucks in front as indicated on the pattern; press the tucks away from the center. Stitch the backs to the front at the shoulders. Clip curves around the neck, turn under all raw edges, and hem. Turn under the raw edges of the back sections and topstitch.

SLEEVES: Cut the sleeves from taffeta. Pleat the top of one sleeve to fit the armhole. Beginning with the center pleat, bring Line A to meet Line B. Continue to make approximately ½-inch pleats on either side of the center pleat, stopping ½ inch from the underarm seam edge. Pin and stitch the sleeve in place. Repeat for the second sleeve.

Make narrow hems in the bottoms of the sleeves. Stitch the underarm seams and side seams of the bodice.

Fit the bodice to the doll, adjust the sleeve length, and sew the narrow lace edge to the cuffs.

JABOT: Cut the corner from a lace handkerchief or select any other decorative piece of lace that is about 4 inches deep for the jabot. Fold under any raw edges and stitch the jabot around the neck from shoulder seam to shoulder seam, gathering if necessary to make a better fit.

SKIRT: Cut an 8x42-inch rectangle of taffeta. Hem one edge. Pin and baste ½-inch-wide vertical pleats in the skirt, fitting the skirt to the bodice as you work. Seam the short ends together; press the pleats in place. Stitch the pleated skirt to the bottom of the bodice. Press the seams toward the bodice and topstitch ⅛ inch from the seam.

SASH: Cut an 11x15-inch piece of taffeta. Fold it in half lengthwise; sew lengthwise, leaving ends open for turning. Turn and press the fabric. Make three pleats across the length of the sash, reducing the sash to 1¾ inches wide. Press. Hand-tack the ends of the sash to each side of the back opening. Add snaps to close. Add bow at back, if desired.

BOOTS: Cut out black felt bottoms and sew together along the curved edge. Turn right side out and slip onto each foot. For the tops, cut pieces from gray vinyl, flopping the pattern over for right and left shoes. Match up A and B seams and stitch. Clip the seams.

Punch small holes with a leather punch or cut slits to make buttonholes as indicated on the pattern. Fit the tops to the legs; mark position for bead buttons and stitch the beads in place. Button tops over legs. Sew black satin bows in place.

Fashion a bow from taffeta; tack the bow to the doll's hair.

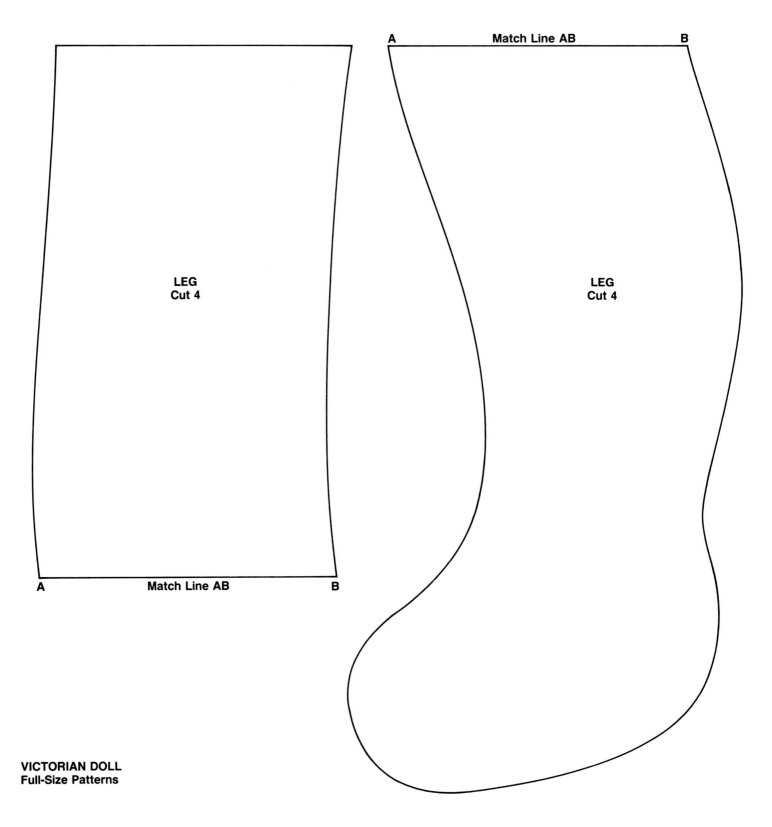

Match Line AB

A   B

LEG
Cut 4

LEG
Cut 4

A   **Match Line AB**   B

VICTORIAN DOLL
Full-Size Patterns

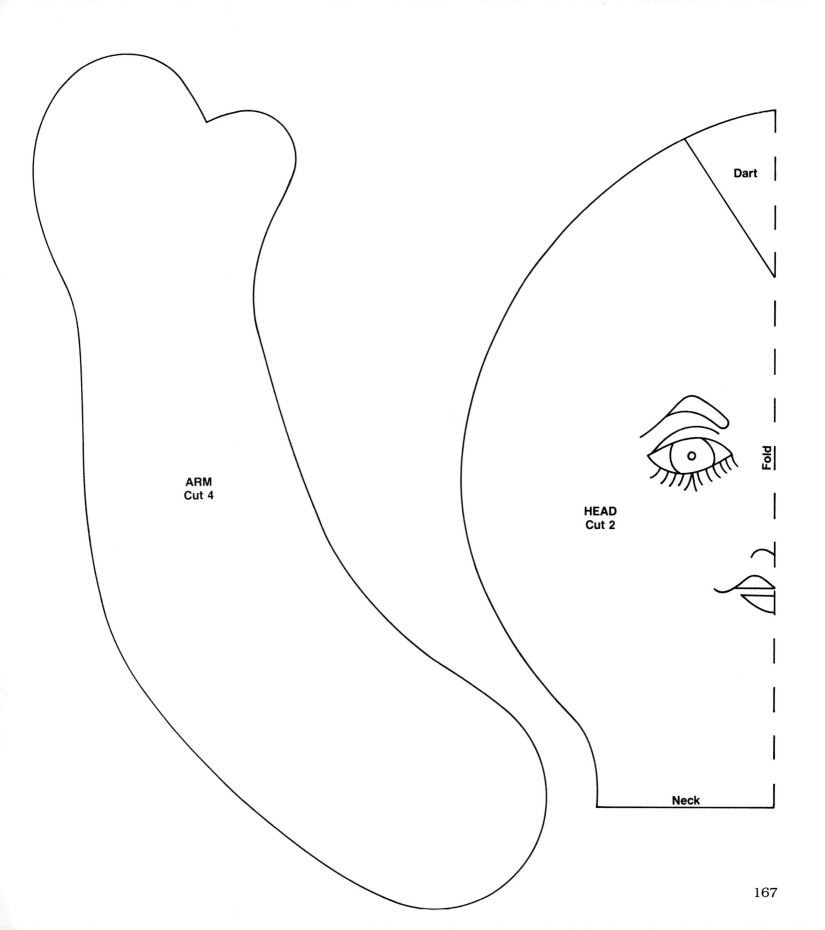

ARM
Cut 4

HEAD
Cut 2

Dart

Fold

Neck

167

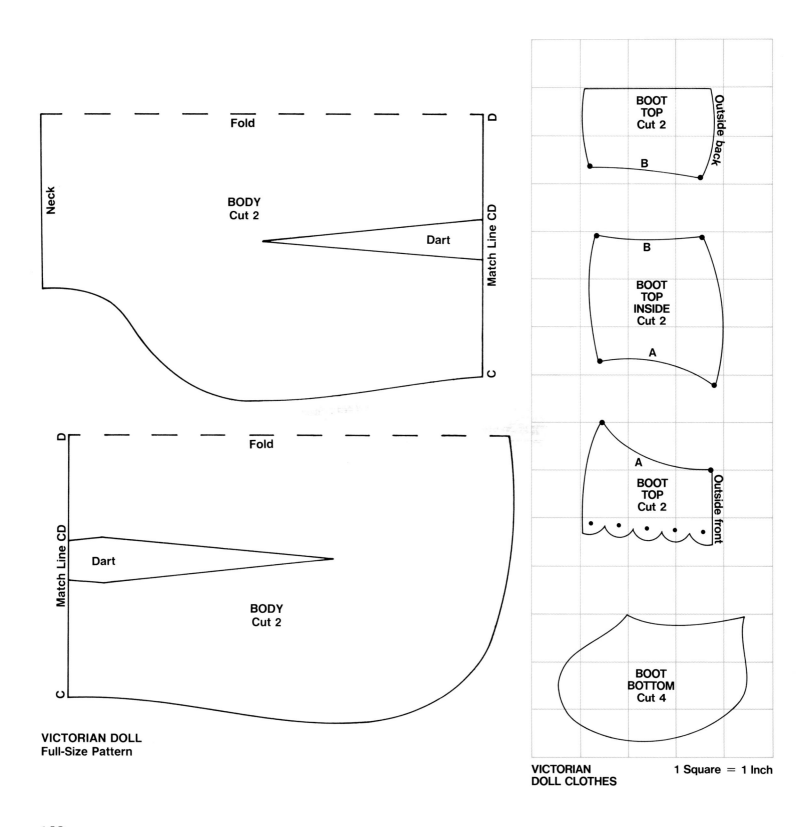

Fold

Neck

BODY
Cut 2

Match Line CD

Dart

D

C

VICTORIAN DOLL
Full-Size Pattern

D

Fold

Match Line CD

Dart

BODY
Cut 2

C

BOOT
TOP
Cut 2

Outside back

B

B

BOOT
TOP
INSIDE
Cut 2

A

A

BOOT
TOP
Cut 2

Outside front

BOOT
BOTTOM
Cut 4

VICTORIAN
DOLL CLOTHES

1 Square = 1 Inch

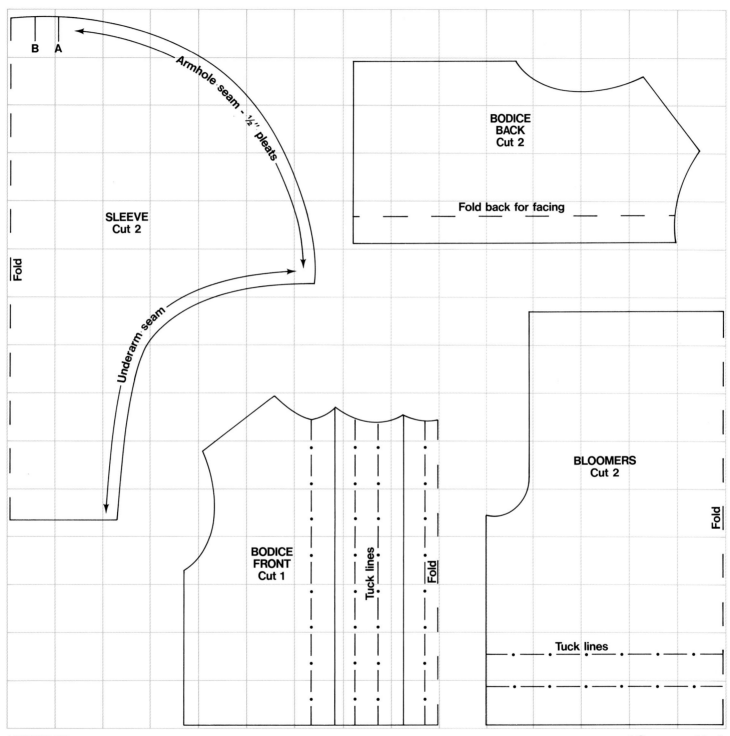

B   A

Armhole seam - ½" pleats

SLEEVE
Cut 2

Underarm seam

Fold

BODICE
BACK
Cut 2

Fold back for facing

BLOOMERS
Cut 2

Fold

BODICE
FRONT
Cut 1

Tuck lines

Fold

Tuck lines

VICTORIAN
DOLL CLOTHES

1 Square = 1 Inch

169

A HOUSEFUL OF HANDMADE TREASURES

Country sentiments often are best expressed in simple statements— strings of popcorn, pieced scraps of fabric, a cozy afghan, and a Yule log burning to warm the winter night.

Bright checkerboards and other stamped ornaments, *right,* fill a tree in no time at all when you get the whole family involved. Kids easily can stamp the designs on cardboard squares and on wooden house and star cutouts. Ask friends to share favorite stories of seasons past while stringing popcorn garlands. Tie the garlands to the tree with colorful plaid satin ribbons.

The chair full of fireside comforts holds patchwork pillows stitched from bits of red and green fabrics.

And when the temperature dips and nights are chilly, the whole family will enjoy this fluffy crocheted afghan. Woven lengths of red and green worsted-weight yarn turn the coverlet into a handsome holiday decoration.

Instructions and patterns for all projects in this chapter begin on page 176.

P resents with personality are a must for a memorable Christmas.

The cuddly stuffed moppet, *opposite,* is a rag doll with a slightly different twist. Machine-stitch the doll from muslin, then stitch over the seams with embroidery floss in a crisscross pattern. Her ragamuffin yarn hairdo and patched calico dress enhance her homespun character.

The herd of corncob reindeer, *below,* looks as if it's not quite sure which direction Santa and Rudolph went.

Make the reindeer from corncobs, twigs, and dowels. Use satin ribbon and jingle bells to add festive collars.

The tiny cross-stitched ornaments, *left,* are worked in two sizes on 18-count even-weave cloth. Hang them on the tree, or fill them with potpourri and tuck them into Christmas stockings.

A HOUSEFUL OF
HANDMADE TREASURES

What could be more fun than crafting old-fashioned garlands of popcorn? Many a contest has taken place in the kitchen or around the fireplace, as family members and friends vie to see who can make the longest popcorn string in the shortest amount of time. The fun comes in hanging the garland on the tree (and in eating the leftovers).

If you'd rather munch popcorn than string it, you can make paper-chain garlands instead.

Children will enjoy stamping evergreen tree and checkerboard designs on gift boxes. Fill one of these containers with homemade bread or cookies for a lovely gift for a holiday-party hostess.

If cross-stitching is one of your favorite techniques, try the Welcome Sampler stitched on natural burlap, *opposite.* An easy-to-read colored pattern appears on pages 184 and 185.

Christmas Afghan

Shown on pages 170 and 171.
Finished size is 65x51 inches.

Abbreviations: See pages 186–187.

MATERIALS
Bernat Berella 4 (100-gram ball):
13 balls of Natural (MC); one ball *each* of No. 8933 red (A) and No. 8982 green (B)
Size J crochet hook or size to obtain gauge given below.

Gauge: 7 hdc = 2 in.

INSTRUCTIONS
With MC ch 228.

Row 1: Hdc in third ch from hook and in each ch across—227 hdc. Ch 2, turn.

Note: In this and all following rows, ch-2 turning ch at beg of row is counted as hdc.

Row 2: Working in back lp only, skip first hdc, hdc in each hdc across, end hdc in turning ch. Ch 2, turn.

Rows 3 and 4: Rep Row 2, ending Row 4 with ch 3, turn.

Row 5: Working in front lp only, * sk 1 hdc, sc in next hdc, ch 3; rep from * across, ending sc in turning ch—114 ch-3 lps. Ch 3, turn.

Row 6: * Hdc in ch-3 lp, ch 1; rep from * across to last ch-3, end hdc in last ch-3 lp—228 hdc. Ch 2, turn.

Row 7: Working in front lp only, sk first hdc, hdc in each rem st across, end hdc in turning ch. Ch 2, turn.

Row 8: Rep Row 2, ending with ch 3.

Row 9: Yo, draw lp through both lps of second hdc, sk 1 hdc, yo and draw lp through both lps of next hdc, yo and draw through all 5 lps on hook for a star st, ch 1 for "eye," * yo and draw lp in same st as last "point" of previous star, sk 1 hdc, yo and draw lp in next hdc, yo and draw through all 5 lps on hook for star st, ch 1 for eye; rep from * across; end hdc in turning ch—113 stars. Ch 3, turn.

Row 10: Yo, draw lp in first eye, yo and draw lp in next eye, yo and draw through all 5 lps on hook for star st, ch 1 for eye, * yo and draw lp in same eye as last point of previous star, yo, draw lp in next eye, yo and draw through all 5 lps on hook for star st, ch 1 for eye, rep from * across, end yo, draw lp in same st as last point of star, yo, draw lp through top of turning ch, yo, draw through all 5 lps on hook, ch 1 for eye—113 stars. Ch 2, turn.

Row 11: Hdc in each eye and star st across, hdc in turning ch—228 hdc. Ch 2, turn.

Rows 12–17: Rep rows 4–9.

Rows 18–24: Rep Row 10, ending rows 18–23 with ch 3, and ending Row 24 with ch 2.

Rows 25–38: Rep rows 3–16, ending Row 16 with ch 2.

Rows 39–52: Rep rows 3–16.

Row 53: Rep Row 9.

Rows 54–68: Rep Row 10, ending rows 54–67 with ch 3 and ending Row 68 with ch 2.

Rows 69–82: Rep rows 25–38.

Rows 83–118: Rep rows 3–38.

Rows 119 and 120: Rep Row 2. Do not fasten off or turn work.

EDGING (for long edges only): Working from left to right, * ch 1, sk 1 st, sc in next st. Rep from * across to opposite corner. Fasten off.

With wrong side facing, join MC to left end of foundation chain. Work as for first side of edging.

TASSELS: Cut MC into 14-inch lengths. Hold 4 pieces tog, fold in half and loop through edge bet pat rows, every other row, skipping lattice rows (rows 5 and 6 = 1 pair of lattice rows).

Cut 48 lengths of A and 24 lengths of B 16 inches longer than lengthwise measurement of afghan. Holding 3 strands of A tog, weave through first 4 pairs of lattice rows. Rep with B through next 4 pairs of lattice rows. Rep with A on last 4 pairs of lattice rows. Tie ends of A and B in overhand knot to look like MC tassels.

House and Star Stamped Ornaments

Shown on pages 170 and 171.
Finished size is 5 inches tall.

MATERIALS
½-inch-thick pine board scraps
Jigsaw
Drill
Small paintbrush
White, blue, yellow, red, green, and gray acrylic paints
Wood scraps or sponge (stamps)

INSTRUCTIONS
Transfer the full-size patterns, *opposite*, onto heavy paper; cut out the shapes. Cut out doors, windows, and trees. Draw around houses on pine and cut out shapes with a jigsaw. Drill holes for hanging the ornaments; sand. Paint the ornaments white, yellow, or blue, referring to the photograph on pages 170 and 171 for guidance. Allow the paint to dry. Use heavy paper templates to draw around windows, doors, and trees on the ornaments.

To stamp decorations
Cut one stamp for each window, door, and tree from wood or sponge.

Place paint on paper plates. Brush paint on the stamps with a paintbrush and press onto the ornaments to fill windows, doors, and trees with color. Dry, then thread hangers through holes to hang.

HOUSE AND STAR STAMPED ORNAMENTS

Full-Size Patterns

Checkerboard Ornament

Shown on pages 170 and 171.
Finished size is 5 inches square.

MATERIALS
5-inch white cardboard square
Red acrylic paint
½-inch-square wood or sponge
 stamp
Nylon cord
Crewel needle
Paper plate

INSTRUCTIONS
Place a small amount of red paint on the paper plate. Dab the end of a ½-inch-square sponge or wood stamp into red paint and practice stamping on a piece of newspaper.

 With light pencil, mark the cardboard square with a ½-inch-square checkerboard pattern (eight squares by eight squares). Stamp the checkerboard pattern with the stamp dipped in red paint. Thread needle with cord, then punch through the corner of the ornament for hanger.

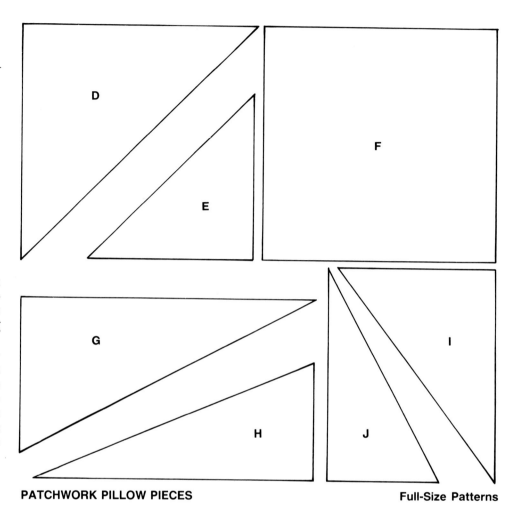

PATCHWORK PILLOW PIECES

Full-Size Patterns

Patchwork Pillows

Shown on pages 170 and 171.
Finished size of the Grandmother's Quilt Pillow is 15x15 inches; Christmas Tree Pillow, 15¾ inches tall; Martha Washington Star Pillow, 10x10 inches.

MATERIALS
For one pillow
½ yard *each* of red, green, and
 white calico
Thread
Polyester fiberfill
Piping
½ yard of calico (pillow backing)

INSTRUCTIONS
GENERAL DIRECTIONS: Read all instructions before beginning. Trace templates from the patterns, *above* and *opposite,* onto cardboard or plastic; add ¼-inch seam allowances all around and cut out. Draw around the cardboard templates on the wrong sides of calico to mark the patchwork pieces. Cut out fabric along drawn lines.

 After the patchwork is completed, pipe the pillow edges, if desired. Cut a piece of calico backing to match the pillow front. With right sides facing, sew front to back ¼ inch from raw edges. Leave an opening for turning and stuffing. Fill pillows with polyes-ter fiberfill and sew closed. (General directions for finishing a pillow appear on page 187.)

For Christmas Tree Pillow
From green calico, cut six G and I pieces, 12 J pieces, and six H pieces. From red calico, cut two G and six *each* of I, J, and H pieces. Cut one 3x4-inch red tree trunk. For star, cut one L and six K pieces from yellow.

 Assemble the patchwork following the piecing diagram, *opposite,* working in horizontal strips across the tree, then assembling the strips into the tree.

continued

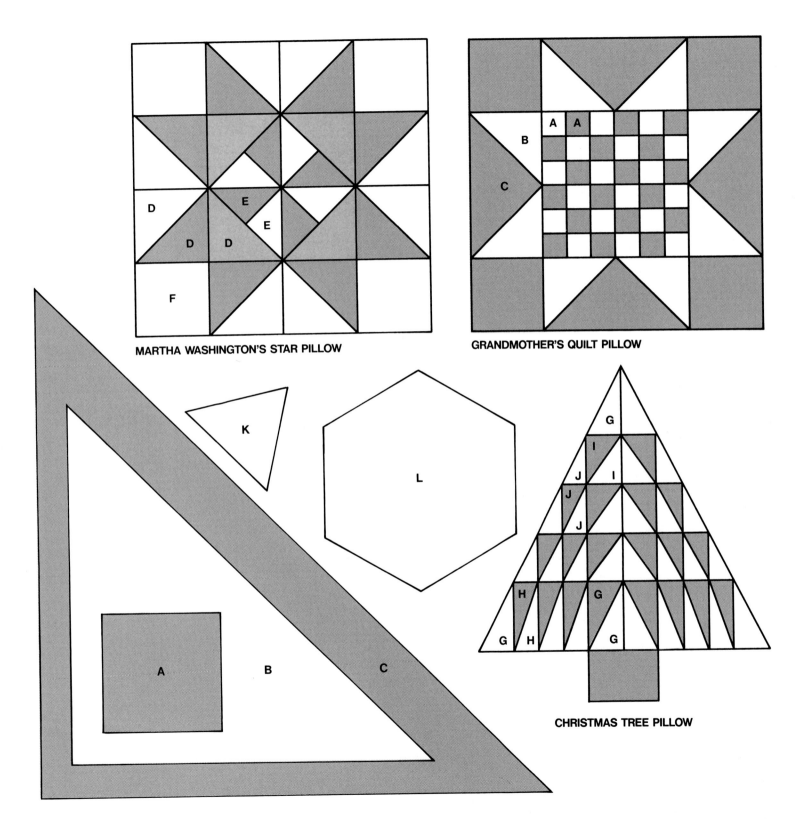

MARTHA WASHINGTON'S STAR PILLOW

GRANDMOTHER'S QUILT PILLOW

CHRISTMAS TREE PILLOW

179

Top Row: Join two green G pieces along long sides to form treetop triangle.

Row 2: Join two green I pieces along long sides to make center triangle. Add a red I to each side of the triangle to make a rectangle. Add a green J triangle to each end of the rectangle.

Row 3: Make the same as for second row. Add a red J triangle to each end of row; add a green J to each end of row.

Row 4: Make the same as for third row. Add a red J triangle to each end of row; add a green J to each end of row.

Row 5: Join two green G pieces along long sides to make center triangle. Add a red G to each side of the triangle to make a rectangle. Add three alternating green and red H triangles to each end of center rectangle. Finish with a green G triangle on each end of row.

For tree trunk, sew long edge of red rectangle at bottom center of fifth row. Assemble rows to make pillow front.

For the star, sew a K triangle along each edge of the center hexagon. Back, then stuff lightly as for pillow.

For Martha Washington Pillow

From red calico, cut four F, eight D, and four E pieces. From white, cut eight D and four E pieces. From green fabric, cut four D pieces.

Lay pieces on flat surface by following the diagram on page 179.

Assemble the patchwork in horizontal strips. Assemble the strips into pillow front.

For Grandmother's Quilt Pillow

From red calico, cut four 4½-inch squares, four C pieces, and 18 A pieces.

From white calico or muslin, cut 18 A pieces and eight B pieces.

COLOR KEY
⊠ Red   ● Green   □ White

CROSS-STITCHED ORNAMENTS

1 Square = 1 Stitch

CHECKED CENTER: Arrange the red and white A squares in a checkerboard design (see the diagram on page 179).

Join the squares to make six rows of six squares each.

Join the rows to complete the center of the pillow.

BORDERS: Join a white B triangle to each side of the four red C triangles, making a total of four rectangles. Press seams.

Join a patched rectangle to two opposite sides of the pillow center. Press the seams.

Add a red 4½-inch square of fabric to both ends of the remaining patched rectangles.

Press seams and join strips to the remaining sides of the pillow front.

Cross-Stitched Ornaments

Shown on page 173.
Finished size of small ornament is 2¼x2¼ inches; large ornament is 4x4 inches.

MATERIALS
One skein *each* of embroidery floss in blue, red, green, and white
Embroidery needle
Embroidery hoop
20-inch square of red 18-count even-weave cloth (makes four large or eight small ornaments)
Green fabric scraps (for ornament backs)
Polyester fiberfill
Monofilament or ribbon (for hanging)

INSTRUCTIONS
Refer to the patterns, *opposite*. Three colors (red, white, and green) are shown on the patterns. To match the blue star ornament in the photograph on page 173, substitute blue for green on the pattern, *opposite*.

Plan placement of ornaments on the cloth. Baste finished dimension of ornaments onto fabric, allowing at least 1 inch between ornaments for seam allowances.

For small ornament
Select star design. Find center of design and center of fabric square. Begin cross-stitching at the center and work outward. Use one ply of floss and work stitches over one thread of the even-weave cloth.

For large ornament
Work large ornament the same as for the small ornament above, except use two plies of floss worked over two threads of the cloth.

Cut around embroidered ornaments, allowing ½ inch for seam allowances. Cut backs from green fabric to match stitched fronts. With right sides facing, machine-stitch around stitchery three threads from stitchery perimeters. Leave openings for turning ornaments right side out. Trim seams, turn, stuff, and sew closed. Attach monofilament or ribbon loops for hanging.

Corncob Reindeer

Shown on pages 173.
Finished reindeer is 9 inches tall.

MATERIALS
For one reindeer
One large corncob
White-painted twigs (antlers)
¼x13-inch dowel
Corn husk; two small bells
15 inches of ¼-inch-wide red ribbon
3 inches of red string
Sandpaper
Hot-glue gun
Saw
Drill with ¼-inch drill bit
Vise

INSTRUCTIONS
Cut the corncob with a saw as follows: Beginning at the round end, cut off a 1¾-inch piece (head). Cut a 2-inch-long neck and a 3½-inch-long body. Using a vise to hold corncob securely, drill four holes on underside of body for legs; drill two holes on top of head for antlers. Cut dowel into four 3¼-inch legs. With a pencil sharpener or knife, sharpen one end of each dowel to a blunt point. Sand opposite ends smooth. Insert pointed ends of legs into body underside and glue in place.

Glue neck to top of body front. Glue head on top of neck. Glue twig antlers into holes on top of head. Cut two ears and a tail from corn husk; glue in place. Thread bells onto string; tie to neck with ribbon.

Country Doll

Shown on page 172.
Finished doll is 17 inches tall.

MATERIALS
½ yard of muslin
½ yard of white printed fabric
½ yard of red paisley fabric
10 yards of off-white bulky yarn (hair)
One 2-inch square *each* of red and green fabric
4 inches of ⅛-inch-wide elastic
Thread
Pink marker
White embroidery floss
Medium gray embroidery floss
9 inches of ecru piping
Polyester fiberfill
Graph paper
Dressmaker's carbon paper

INSTRUCTIONS
Patterns on pages 182 and 183 are full size. *Note:* Patterns include ¼-inch seams.

Cut pattern pieces as follows: body parts from muslin; dress bodice, sleeves, and a 12x45-inch skirt from white print; 10x16-inch apron front, two 1½x5-inch apron straps, and a 1½x12-inch waistband from red paisley fabric.

For the doll
FACE: First stitch the two face pieces, right sides together, along the center seam. Matching the center seam of the fabric to the center seam of the pattern, transfer the embroidery lines to the face with dressmaker's carbon paper.

continued

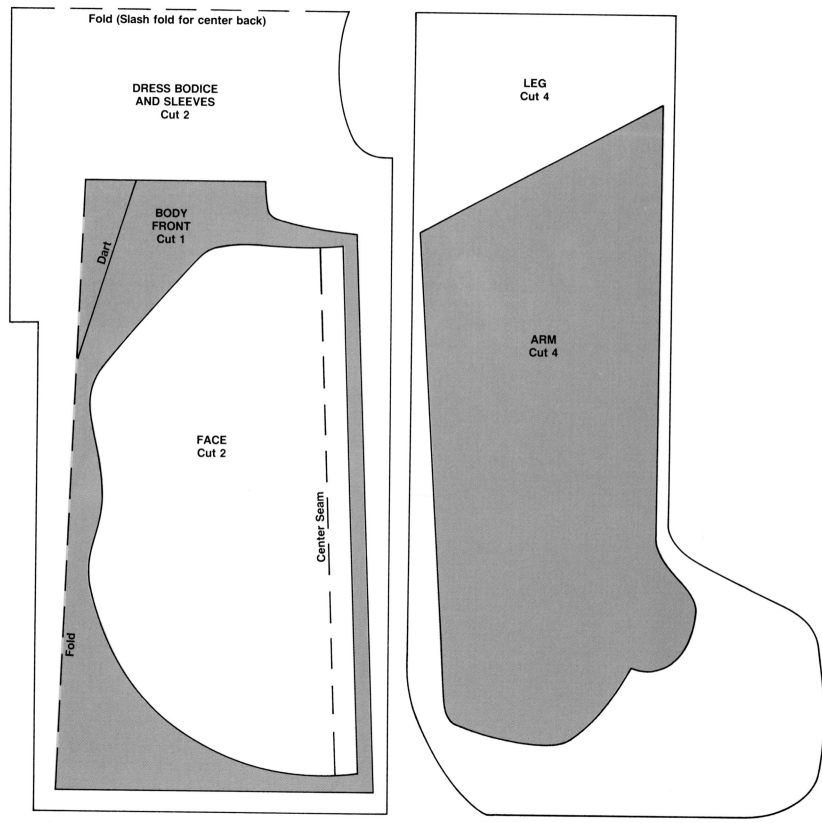

Fold (Slash fold for center back)

DRESS BODICE
AND SLEEVES
Cut 2

LEG
Cut 4

BODY
FRONT
Cut 1

Dart

FACE
Cut 2

Center Seam

Fold

ARM
Cut 4

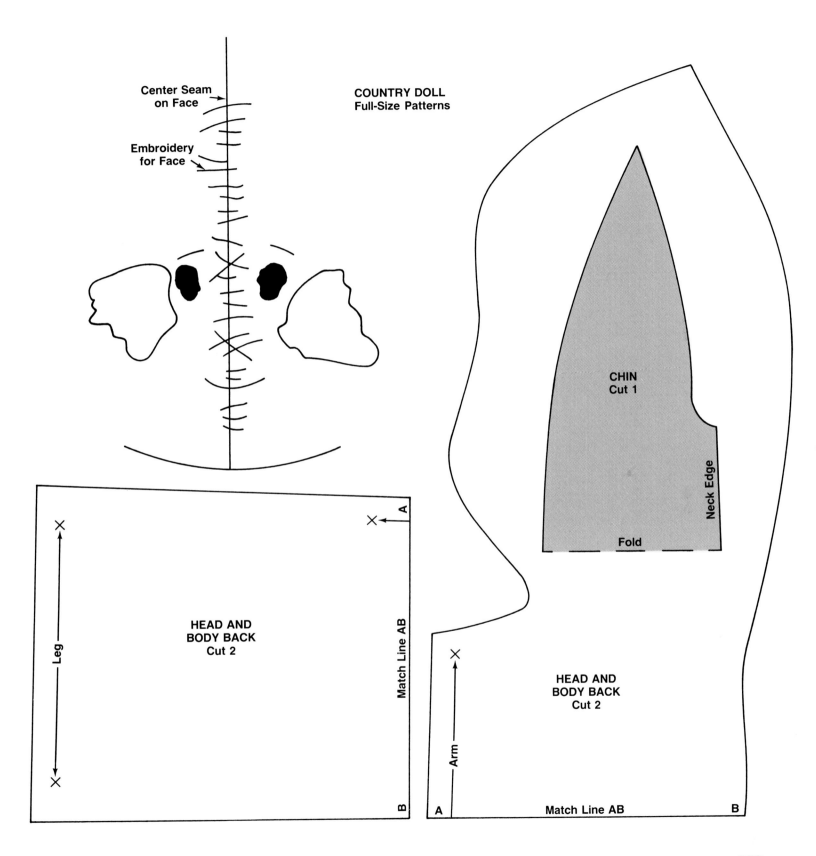

Center Seam
on Face

Embroidery
for Face

COUNTRY DOLL
Full-Size Patterns

CHIN
Cut 1

Neck Edge

Fold

HEAD AND
BODY BACK
Cut 2

Leg

Match Line AB

A

B

HEAD AND
BODY BACK
Cut 2

Arm

A   Match Line AB   B

183

Embroider the eyes, mouth, and stitches along the center seam with two plies of gray floss. Embroider using outline or stem stitches. (See stitch diagrams on page 186.) Color cheeks with a pink marker.

BODY/HEAD: On the body front, stitch the dart as indicated. With right sides together, match the neck edges of the chin and body front; stitch. Pin the curved edge of the chin to the face, right sides facing, matching the chin fold line to the center seam of the face. Stitch. With right sides facing, pin the two head and body pieces together along the center back seam; stitch. Sew the doll body/head back to the front, right sides facing, easing curves and leaving the bottom open. Clip curves and trim seams. Turn the body right side out and stuff it firmly. Sew the bottom closed.

ARMS AND LEGS: Sew the arm and leg backs to the fronts, right sides together, and stitch, leaving the top of each open. Trim seams, clip curves, and turn. Stuff, then slip-stitch openings closed. Sew the arms and legs to the body where indicated on the pattern.

HAIR: Cut the yarn into 6-inch lengths. Separate the lengths into eight bunches; wrap thread around the center of each bunch and tack to the head.

For the clothing

DRESS: Sew the bodice and sleeve pieces together along the shoulders and underarms, right sides facing. Slash the back along the length of the fold line.

Fold under ¼ inch on the raw edges of the bottoms of the sleeves and tuck a 2-inch length of elastic

COLOR KEY

■ Christmas-Red 971 ▨ Mustard 712 ▨ Cobalt Blue 544

under the seam allowance on each. Pulling the elastic taut while you sew, stitch through the seam allowance and elastic. This will gather the bottoms of the sleeves. Sew the short sides of the skirt together, right sides facing, leaving the seam open 2 inches at one end. This seam will be the center back seam, and the opening will be at the top of the back.

Hem the skirt bottom and gather the top edge to fit the bodice waist. With right sides facing, sew the skirt to the bodice, matching the back openings. Trim the bodice neck with

ecru piping. Put the dress on the doll and sew the back openings closed, tucking all raw edges inside and catching the back of the doll in the stitches.

APRON: Finish the short sides of the apron front with rolled hems and stitch a 1-inch hem along one long edge. Using white floss and long, straight stitches, sew the fabric-square patches to the apron front. Gather the upper edge of the apron front until it is 5 inches long.

■ **Khaki-Brown 451**   ■ **Hunter-Green 614**   ■ **Christmas-Green 696**

1 Square = 1 Stitch

Shown on pages 174 and 175.

INSTRUCTIONS

Measure and mark checkerboard squares on the container lid. Cut a wood scrap with an end to match the size of one checkerboard square. Place red paint on a paper plate and dab the square end of the wood scrap into the paint. Stamp the checkerboard on the lid.

For the surrounding green forest border, cut a triangular stamp (tree) from wood. Stamp the trees around the checkerboard. With a paintbrush, paint tree trunks.

Welcome Sampler

Shown on pages 174 and 175.
Finished size is 14½x24 inches.

MATERIALS

21x30-inch piece of ecru burlap (available at fabric stores)
Paternayan three-ply wool in the following colors and amounts: 20 yards of No. 971 Christmas red; 2 yards of No. 544 cobalt blue; 1 yard of No. 712 mustard; 10 yards of No. 451 khaki brown; 4 yards of No. 614 hunter green; 15 yards of No. 696 Christmas green
Crewel needle
Embroidery hoop

INSTRUCTIONS

Refer to the graph, *above,* for stitching the sampler. Find the center of the design and the center of the burlap; begin stitching here.

Thread crewel needle with one ply of yarn and stitch the cross-stitches over two threads of the burlap fabric.

When the stitchery is complete, press the sampler and frame it as desired.

Center the waistband strip over the apron front, right sides together. Stitch. Fold under the raw edges of the waistband; press. Wrap the waistband around the doll and tack in place, catching the doll in the stitches. Fold the raw edges of the shoulder straps to the inside along the long edges; press. Topstitch close to the edges of the straps. Position the straps over the doll's shoulders, tucking the ends under the waistband in the front and back; stitch.

Checkerboard Game Box

Shown on pages 174 and 175.

MATERIALS

Lidded container
Red and green acrylic paints
Wood scraps
Paintbrush

Embroidery Stitches

Buttonhole Stitch

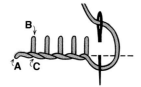

Chain Stitch

Couched Filling Stitch

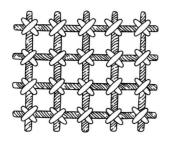

Couching Stitch

Darning Stitch

Featherstitch

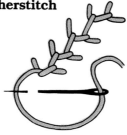

French Knot

Long-and-Short Stitch

Outline (or Seam) Stitch

Parallel Featherstitch

Satin Stitch

Needlepoint Stitches

Bargello Stitch

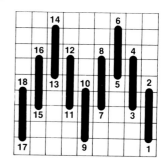

Basket-Weave Stitch

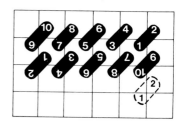

Continental Stitch

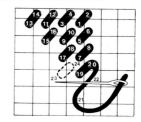

Cross-Stitch

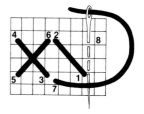

Crocheting Abbreviations

```
beg ...................................begin(ning)
ch ................................................ chain
cl ............................................... cluster
dc ...............................double crochet
lp(s) ....................................loop(s)
pc ...........................................popcorn
rep ............................................. repeat
sc ............................... single crochet
sk ...............................................skip
sl st .......................................slip stitch
sp ..............................................space
st(s) .........................................stitch(es)
* ................repeat from * as indicated
```

Knitting Abbreviations

```
dec ........................................... decrease
inc ...........................................increase
k ...................................................... knit
p ......................................................purl
pat ............................................ pattern
rem ........................................remaining
rep ............................................. repeat
rnd ..............................................round
sk ...............................................skip
sl st .......................................slip stitch
st(s) ....................................... stitch(es)
tog ...........................................together
yo ..........................................yarn over
* ................repeat from * as indicated
```

Finishing Pillows and Sachets

To assemble a pillow or sachet without adding trims to the edges, simply mark the finished size on the wrong side of the stitchery. Pin a piece of backing fabric to the stitchery, right sides facing. Stitch along the outline, leaving an opening for turning. Trim the seams, turn the work, and press. Stuff with fiberfill to desired firmness. Slip-stitch the opening closed.

RUFFLES AND PIPING: Cut the ruffle or piping strips on the straight grain or on the bias. The choice depends on the nature of the project. Cut plain fabric on the bias—ruffles will be more graceful and piping will be easier to shape. Crosswise-cut straight-grain strips are somewhat easier to handle than those cut lengthwise.

To make ruffles, cut fabric into strips that are twice the width of the finished size *plus* twice the width of the seam allowance. (Use ½-inch seams for large items like pillows and ¼-inch seams for smaller items.) The length of the strip should be at least twice the finished length of the edge to which it will be stitched. Cut strips, seam ends to form a circle, then fold in half lengthwise, keeping the edges even; press. Machine-stitch two rows (with longest stitch setting) through both thicknesses; stitch one row directly on the seam line and the second row evenly between first row and raw edge. Pull bobbin threads to gather.

For piping, wrap a strip of fabric around cording; baste raw edges together. (Do not baste snugly against cording at this point.) Trim seam allowance to match that of ruffle.

It's easiest to apply the piping and/or ruffles to the right side of the stitchery before further assembly.

Cut away excess fabric to form the same seam allowance as for piping or ruffle. Pin the piping or ruffle to the right side of the work, keeping the raw edges even with the edge of the stitchery. The folded edge of the ruffle and the rolled corded edge of the piping will face the center of the stitchery, with the raw edges of both facing outward. Evenly distribute the ruffle's fullness, with some extra fullness at the corners to prevent the ruffle from cupping. Baste the piping/ruffle directly over the seam line. Complete as you would for the untrimmed pillow, *above*.

CREDITS

We would like to express our gratitude and appreciation to the many people who helped us with this book.

Our special thanks to the following designers who enthusiastically contributed projects and ideas.

Thanks, also, to the photographers, whose creative talents and technical skills added much to this book. In addition, we acknowledge our debt to the companies, institutions, and individuals who provided materials, locations for photography, or in some other way contributed to this book.

Designers

Jennifer Baker—6-7, vest and table runner

Susan Bates—156-157, album cover, tablecloth; 159, album cover

Jan Bishop—68-69

Taresia Boernke—142-143, doll; 144; 159, doll

Ruth Bouseman—18-19, framed floral ornaments

Coats and Clark—109; 123

Deborah Collins—20, sampler

Laurie Craven—11; 142-143, cross-stitch ornament; 158

Phyllis Dunstan—71, cat and dog toys; 173, reindeer

Pam Dyer—9; 50-51, trees and reindeer

Pam Elifritz—156-157, Christmas balls, picture mats; 159, picture mat

Dixie Falls—130-131; 132-133

Barb Forbes—22-23

Jacky Garlock—20-21, angel

Sandy Gregor for Tahki—106-107, man's sweater

Linda Hermanstorfer—52

Hmong Handworks—173, cross-stitch ornaments

Claudia and Carroll Hopf—82-83

Joanne Hurley—35, wooden angel

Amy Jerdee—170-171, tree ornaments; 174-175, box

Rebecca Jerdee—20, fabric swag and Joy hearth hanging; 172; 174-175, sampler

Juene Johnson—86-87, sampler; 89

Marjorie Wedge Mable—120-121, firecrackers

Stacey Malloy—142-143, wooden ornaments

Sandy Moran—18-19, miniature hat ornaments

Joan Moshimer—53, hooked rug

Nancy Antisdel Nielsen—3; 30-31, muslin Santas, Santa and paper heart ornaments; 32-33; 35, Santa ornament; 86-87, copper tulips, duck and rabbit boxes; 88; 91, tulip ornaments

Jean Norman—6-7, ornaments; 8, ornaments; 91, angel

Sally Paul—50-51, place mats; 54-55

Kay and Clarence Payne—120-121, flags, Uncle Sams, soldiers, drums, bandboxes; 122, bandboxes, Uncle Sam

Liz Porter—30-31, star pillow on rocker, table covering; 34, octagonal string star pillow and wall hanging

Beverly Rivers—142-143, patchwork projects; 145

Helene Rush for Reynolds—111, sweater jacket and hat

Joyce Shelton—170-171, afghan

Margaret Sindelar—10; 70,
   pajamas; 90, dress

Rosa Snyder—142-143, floorcloth

Simpson Southwick—108

Cecilia Sreshta—106-107,
   woman's sweater

Betty Waters—35, stockings and
   Santas on mantel

Sue Welsh—170-171, patchwork
   pillows

Dee Wittmack—46-47, samplers;
   53, needlepoint cat

Photographers

Sean Fitzgerald—3, 11, 32-33, 50-
   51, 52-53, 71 (bottom), 89, 92-
   93, 120-121, 122, 133, 156-157,
   158-159

Hopkins Associates—10, 20-21

Michael Jensen—6-7, 9, 18-19,
   30-31, 34, 35 (bottom), 46-47,
   68-69, 70, 71 (top), 82-83, 86-
   87, 88, 90-91, 106-107, 108-
   109, 110-111, 123, 131 (detail)

Scott Little—8, 22-23, 35 (top),
   54-55, 106 (inset), 130-131,
   132, 142-143, 144-145, 170-
   171, 172-173, 174-175

Acknowledgments

Aarlan Yarn Company
   128 Smith Pl.
   Cambridge, MA 02138

Astor Place
   239 Main Ave.
   Stirling, NJ 07980

C.M. Offray & Son, Inc.
   261 Madison Ave.
   New York, NY 10016

Coats & Clark, Inc.
   P.O. Box 1010
   Toccoa, GA 30577

Dan River Fabrics
   111 W. 40th St.
   New York, NY 10018

DMC Corporation
   107 Trumbull St.
   Elizabeth, NJ 07206

Steven and Michelle Doss

Dot's Frame Shoppe
   4521 Fleur Dr.
   Des Moines, IA 50321

Mr. and Mrs. Jim Forbes

Habersham Plantation Corp.
   P.O. Box 1209
   Toccoa, GA 30577

Phila Hach
   Hachland Hills Bed & Breakfast
   1601 Madison St.
   Clarksville, TN 37040

Ron Hawbaker

Heritage Imports
   P.O. Box 328
   Pella, IA 50219

Dr. and Mrs. Joe Holt

Jack Hughes, Woodcarver
   Box 329
   Tilghman, MD 21671

Jan Laurel

MPR Assoc.
   "Creative Twist"
   P.O. Box 7343
   High Point, NC 27264

Mr. and Mrs. Jim Menees

Pat Millin

Joan Moshimer
   Craftsman Hooked Rugs
   Kennebunkport, ME 04046

P & B Fabrics, Inc.
   898 Mahler Rd.
   Burlingame, CA 94010

Linda Parlier

Liz Porter

Don Sires

Laura Sumner

Susan Bates, Inc.
   212 Middlesex Ave.
   Chester, CT 06412

Tom Thompson

Waverly Fabrics and Wallcoverings
   Division of Schumacher & Co.
   79 Madison Ave.
   New York, NY 10016

Jack West

Don Wipperman

Linda Youngquist

Zweigart Fabrics and Canvas
   Cross-Stitch Miracles
   P.O. Box 132282
   Euclid, OH 44132

INDEX

For photographs, see pages noted in **bold** type; remaining numbers refer to instructions pages.

Have BETTER HOMES AND GARDENS® magazine delivered to your door. For information, write to:
MR. ROBERT AUSTIN
P.O. BOX 4536
DES MOINES, IA 50336